¡Viva el español!

Workbook

System A

John De Mado
Linda West Tibensky
Patti Lozano

Jane Jacobsen-Brown
Christine Wolinski Szeszol
Donna Alfredo Wardanian

Marcela Gerber, Series Consultant

The McGraw·Hill Companies

www.WrightGroup.com

Copyright ©2005 Wright Group/McGraw-Hill

All rights reserved. Except as permitted under the United States Copyright Act, no part of this publication may be reproduced or distributed in any form or by any means, or stored in a database or retrieval system, without the prior written permission from the publisher, unless otherwise indicated.

Printed in the United States of America.

Send all inquiries to:
Wright Group/McGraw-Hill
P.O. Box 812960
Chicago, Illinois 60681

ISBN: 0-07-602952-2

7 8 9 10 POH 11 10 09 08

The McGraw-Hill Companies

Contenido

Nombre ______________________

Lección 1

¡Hola! ¿Cómo te llamas?

Yo aprendo el vocabulario

Más vocabulario

¿Cómo se llama el niño?	Se llama José.
¿Cómo se llama la niña?	Se llama Elena.
¿Cómo te llamas?	Me llamo Juan.

Nombre ____________________

Yo hablo

Your class is creating a photo gallery. Draw a picture of yourself inside this frame. Write your name on the line at the bottom. Then say your name to a classmate and ask what his or her name is.

Me llamo ____________________.

Nombre ____________________

Yo practico

A. Circle the best answer.

1. Buenos días.

2. Buenas tardes.

3. Buenas noches.

4. Hasta la vista.

5. La rana.

6. Me llamo Elena.

Nombre ______________________

B. Pedro has just moved to your town. He has many questions about the people he sees. Circle the picture that best answers each question.

1. ¿Cómo se llama el niño?

Tina

Martín

Ramona

2. ¿Cómo se llama la niña?

Ramona

Martín

Tina

3. ¿Cómo se llama la señora?

Ramona

señor Fuentes

señora Ayala

4. ¿Cómo se llama el señor?

señor Fuentes

señora Ayala

Ramona

5. ¿Cómo te llamas?

____

Draw a picture of yourself and a friend. Share it with the class.

Nombre ______________________

Yo juego

Can you get to the ice cream store first? You may play this game alone or with a partner. Many people will talk to you on your way from your house to the ice cream store. You must stop and answer each person correctly before going on. If you respond correctly, you may take another turn. When you come to a person who says nothing, you must start the conversation.

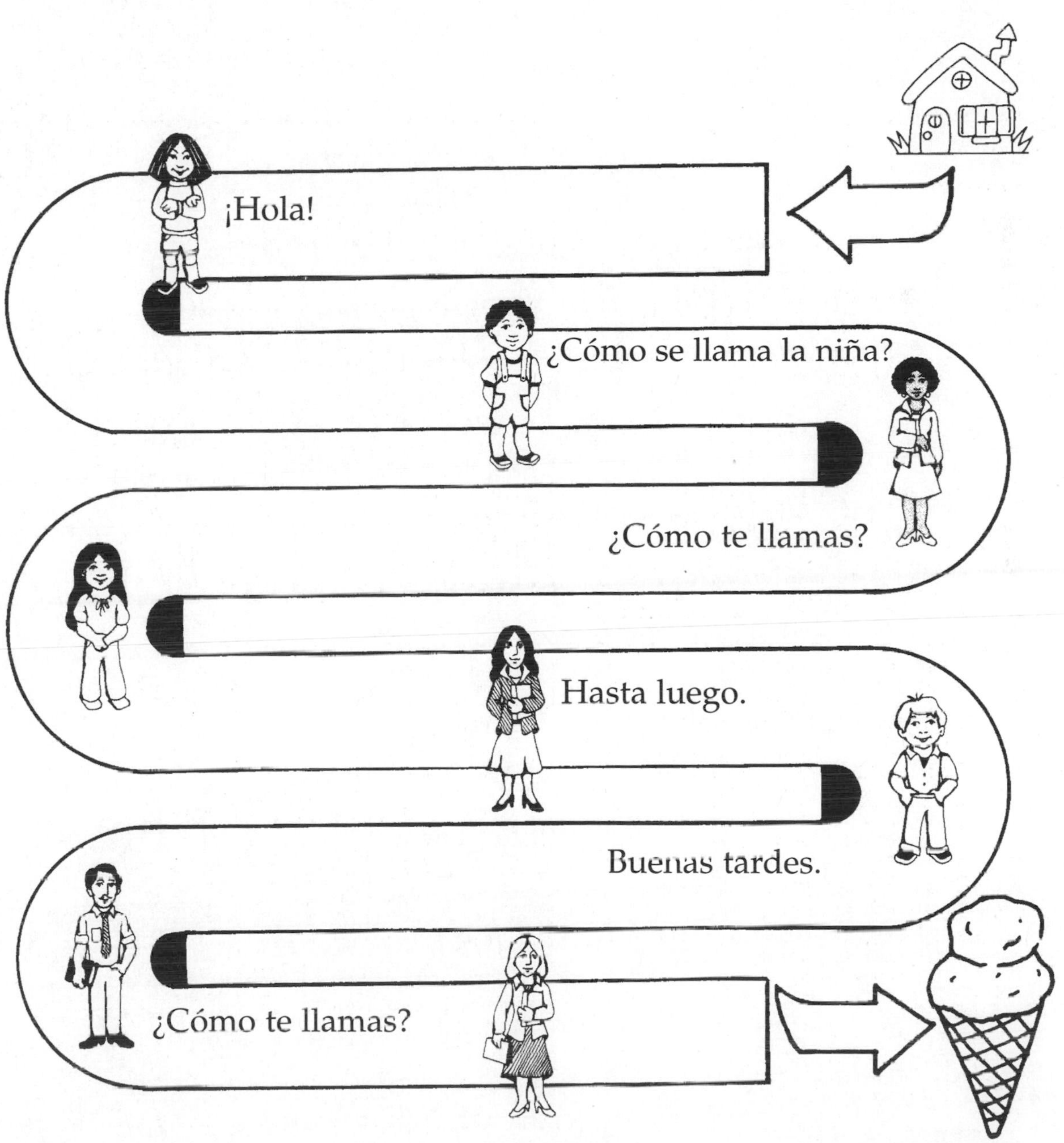
¡Hola!
¿Cómo se llama la niña?
¿Cómo te llamas?
Hasta luego.
Buenas tardes.
¿Cómo te llamas?

Nombre ______________________________

Yo imagino

Draw a picture of some of your friends in the space below.

Share your picture with the class. They will say **¿Cómo se llama el niño?, ¿Cómo se llama la niña?** or **Muéstrame a ___________.** Answer your classmates' questions.

Nombre ______________________

Lección 2

Vamos a mirar alrededor de nuestro salón de clases

Yo aprendo el vocabulario

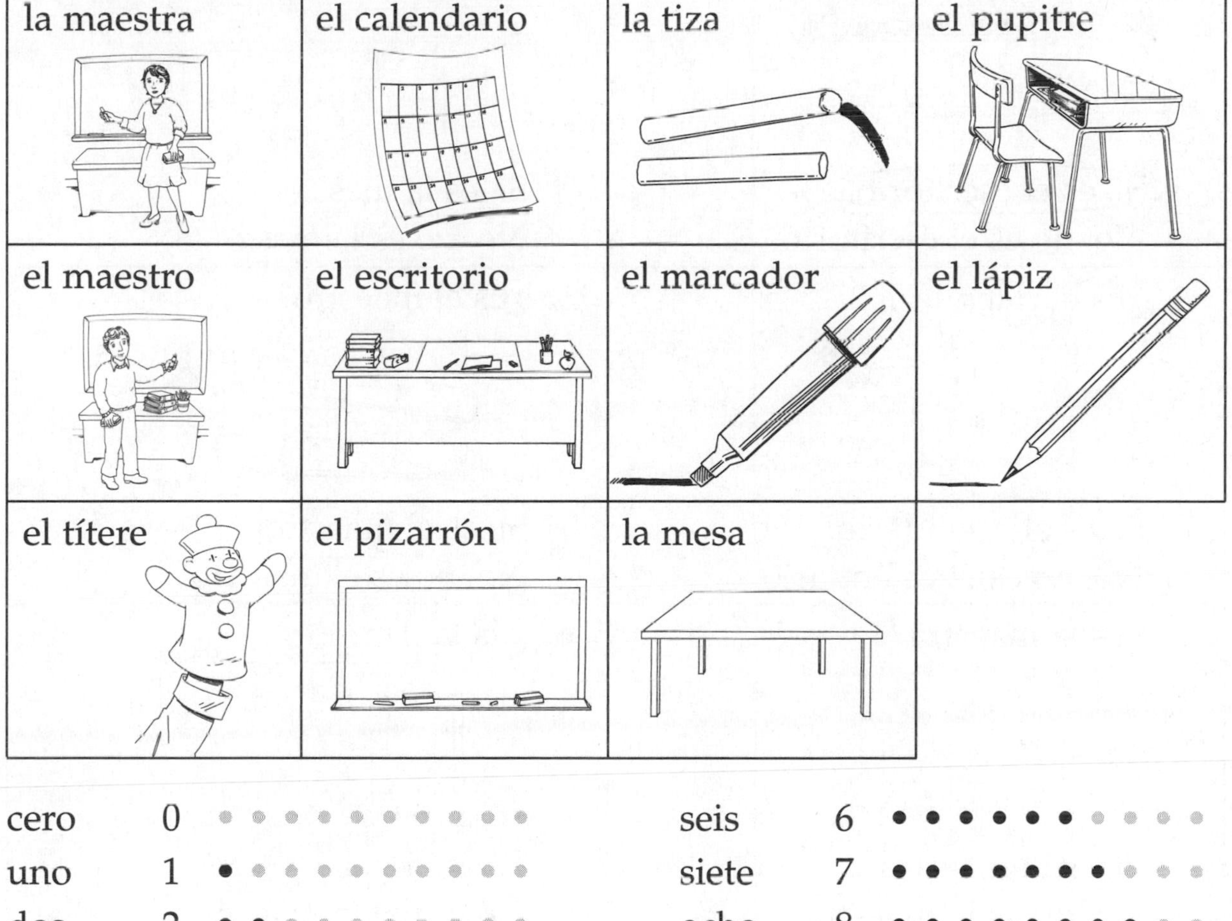

cero	0		seis	6	
uno	1	•	siete	7	• • • • • • •
dos	2	• •	ocho	8	• • • • • • • •
tres	3	• • •	nueve	9	• • • • • • • • •
cuatro	4	• • • •	diez	10	• • • • • • • • • •
cinco	5	• • • • •			

Más vocabulario

¿Es ____?	Sí, es ____.	el
¡Hasta mañana!	No, no es _____.	la

Nombre ______________________

Yo hablo

It's Pedro's first day at school. Everything is new to him, and he has many questions. Answer his questions. First, look at the picture. Then say whether or not it is the object Pedro is asking about. Circle your answer. Follow the example.

Example: ¿Es el escritorio? 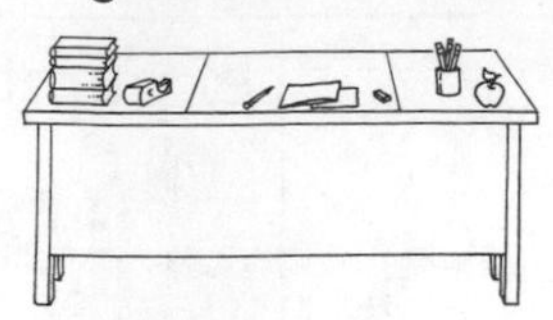 (Sí, es el escritorio.) No, no es el escritorio.	**4.** ¿Es la mesa? 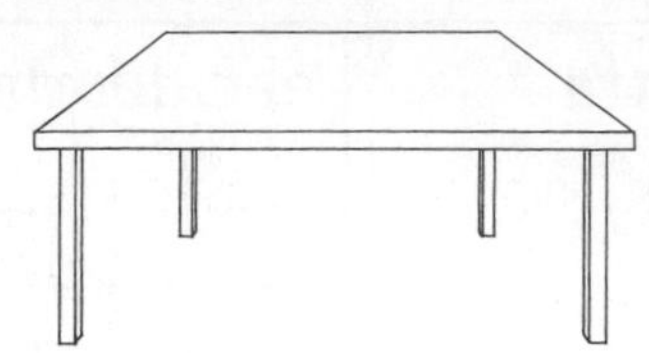 Sí, es la mesa. No, no es la mesa.
1. ¿Es el calendario? 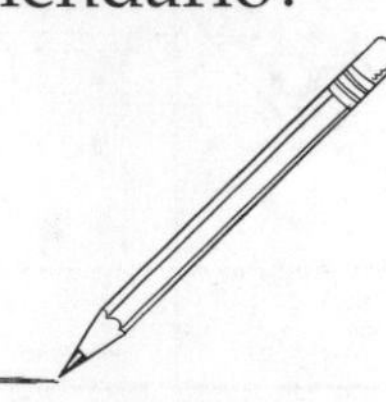 Sí, es el calendario. No, no es el calendario.	**5.** ¿Es el maestro? 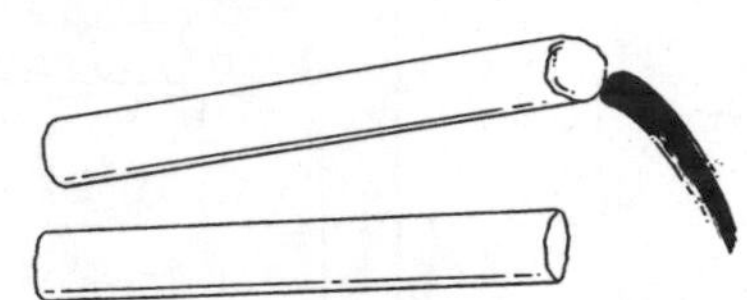 Sí, es el maestro. No, no es el maestro.
2. ¿Es la maestra?  Sí, es la maestra. No, no es la maestra.	**6.** ¿Es la tiza? 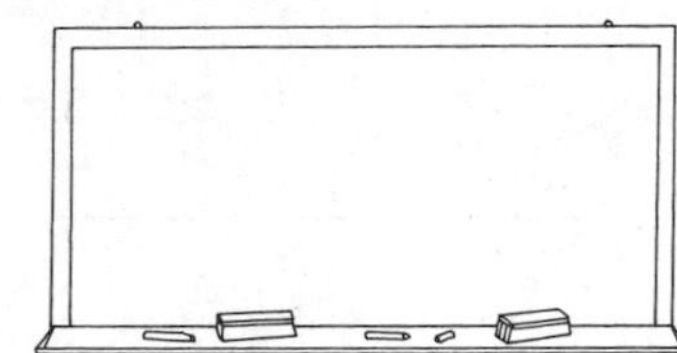 Sí, es la tiza. No, no es la tiza.
3. ¿Es el lápiz? 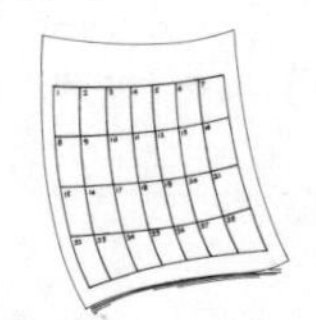 Sí, es el lápiz. No, no es el lápiz.	**7.** ¿Es el pizarrón?  Sí, es el pizarrón. No, no es el pizarrón.

Nombre ______________________________

Yo practico

Help your teacher count the number of items in the classroom. Listen to the questions and write the correct number in each space.

1. ¿Cuántos pizarrones hay en la clase?

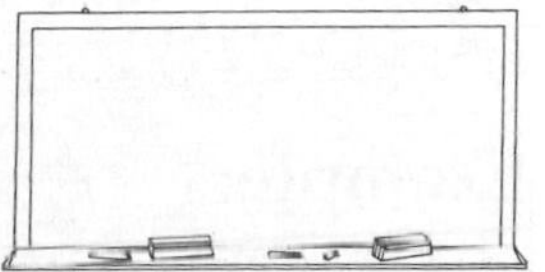

____

2. ¿Cuántos calendarios hay en la clase?

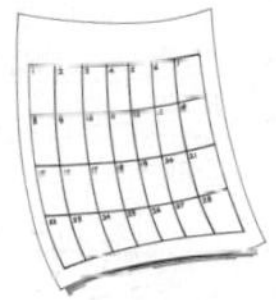

____

3. ¿Cuántas mesas hay en la clase?

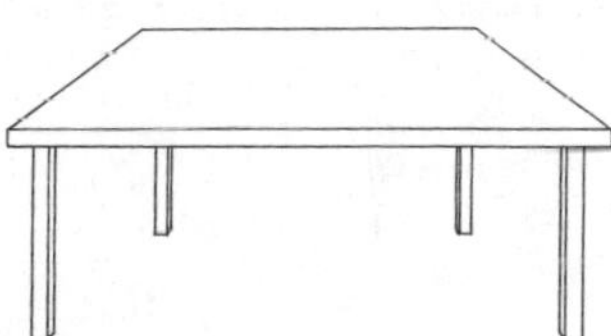

____

4. ¿Cuántos títeres hay en la clase?

____

5. ¿Cuántos lápices hay en el escritorio?

____

6. ¿Cuántas tizas hay en el pizarrón?

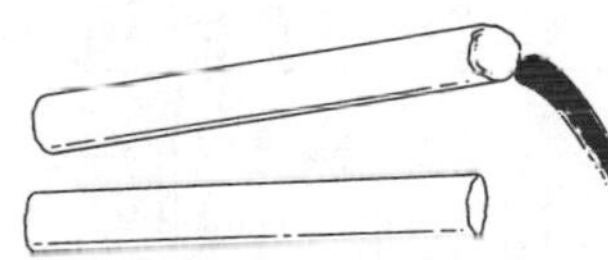

____

7. ¿Cuántos marcadores hay en tu pupitre?

____

Nombre ______________________________

Yo juego

Look at the picture at the bottom of this page. Circle the objects there that you can name. Then count each item that you have circled and write its name and number next to its picture. Follow the example.

Example: 

una maestra

1. ______________________________
2. ______________________________
3. ______________________________
4. ______________________________
5. ______________________________
6. ______________________________
7. 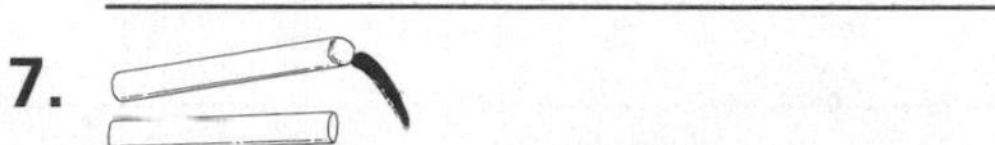 ______________________________
8. 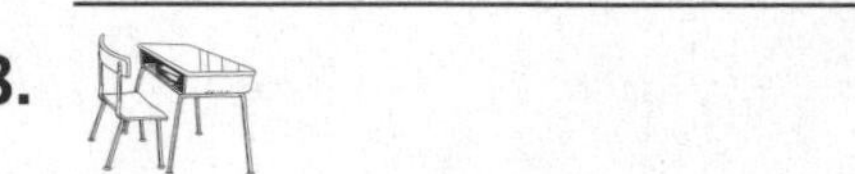 ______________________________
9. 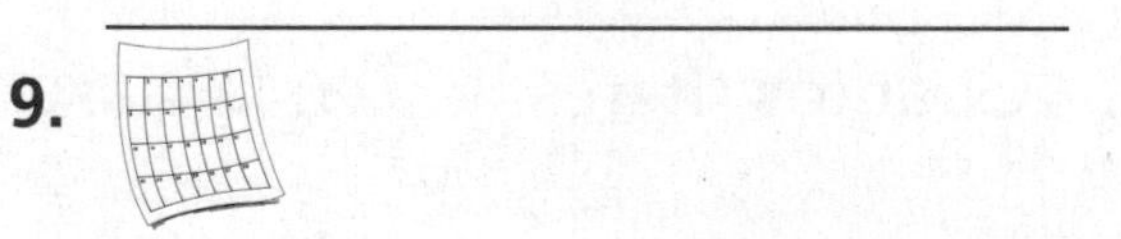 ______________________________
10.  ______________________________

Nombre ______________________________

Yo imagino

A. Pretend that your teacher has sent a note home to your parents to tell them about your classroom. Color the number of objects you hear your teacher read.

1. dos pizarrones

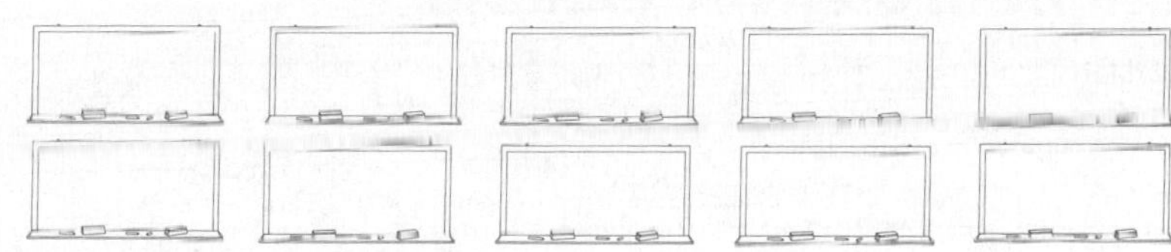

2. seis marcadores

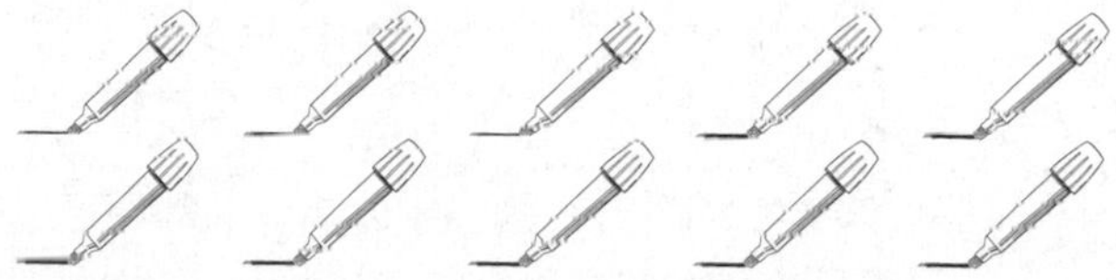

3. diez títeres

4. cero mesas

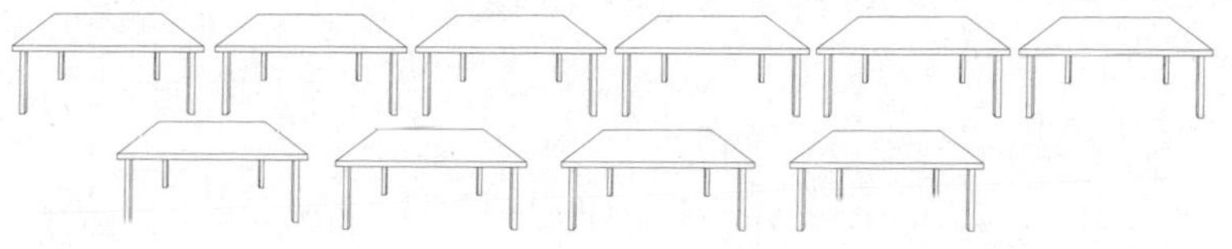

5. cuatro tizas

6. ocho lápices

7. cinco pupitres

B. It's a new school year and *you* are the teacher. On a separate sheet of paper, draw your classroom. You have ten children in your class. Fill your room with objects you can name in Spanish. When your drawing is finished, show it to a friend and talk about it with him or her.

Nombre ______________________________

Lección 3

¿Qué más hay en el salón de clases?

Yo aprendo el vocabulario

Más vocabulario

¿Cómo estás?
Estoy (muy) bien.
Estoy (muy) mal.
Estoy así, así.
Estoy más o menos.
¡Hasta luego!

Nombre ______________________

Yo hablo

Your new neighbor señora Sánchez has stopped by to visit. She is asking about school and your classroom. Take turns answering her questions.

1. ¿Cómo estás?
2. ¿Estás muy mal?
3. ¿Cómo te llamas?
4. ¿Cuántos globos hay en la clase?
5. ¿Cuántos relojes hay en la clase?
6. ¿Cuántos mapas hay en la clase?
7. ¿Cuántas banderas hay en la clase?
8. ¿Cuántas sillas hay en la clase?
9. ¿Cuántas computadoras hay en la clase?
10. ¿Cuántos libros hay en tu escritorio?
11. ¿Cuántos creyones tienes?
12. ¿Cuántos lápices tienes?

Nombre ______________________

Yo practico

A. You are a teacher getting ready for the beginning of the school year. There's a big sale at the store and you are shopping for school supplies. What classroom objects do you see in the store window? Look at the pictures and take turns saying the names of the objects that you see.

B. How do these children feel today? Look at their faces. Then take turns saying how they feel.

Nombre ______________________________

Yo juego

It is time to go outside for recess. Can you name each item you see on the way to the door? Say the name of each item along the path out loud. See who can make it all the way to the playground.

Nombre ______________________________

Yo imagino

There is life in a faraway galaxy, and alien children go to school just like earth children! What do the alien children look like? Use your imagination to draw one. Then draw his or her classroom and the objects in it. Finally, take turns talking about your picture with the rest of the class.

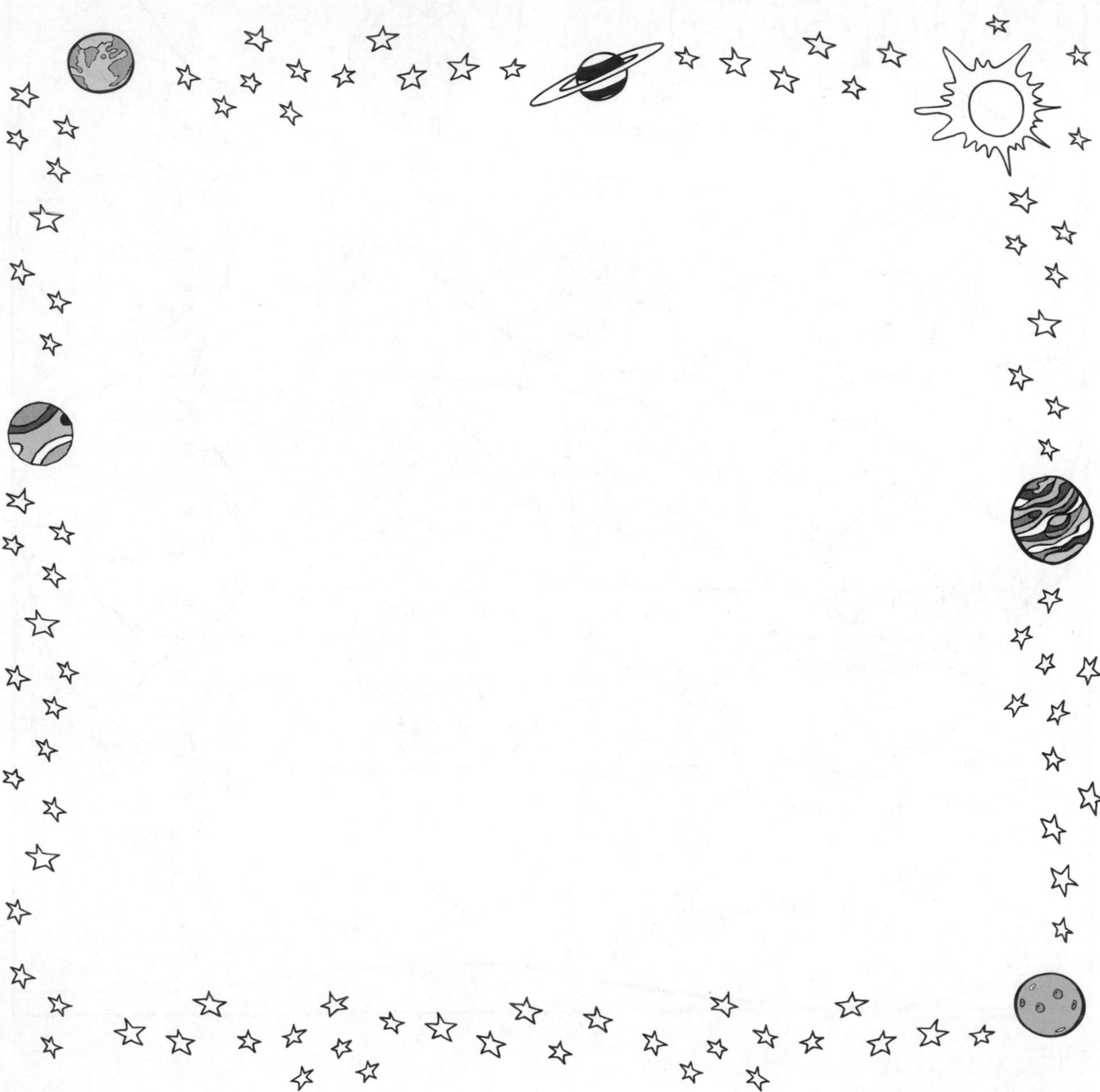

Nombre ________________

Lección 4

¿De qué color es?

Yo aprendo el vocabulario

el color / los colores

○ rojo

○ blanco

○ azul

○ negro

○ amarillo

○ verde

○ marrón

○ rosado

○ gris

○ morado

○ anaranjado

Los días de la semana

lunes	martes	miércoles	jueves	viernes	sábado	domingo

Más vocabulario

¿Qué día es hoy?
Hoy es martes.

Nombre ______________________________

Yo hablo

You will need colored pencils or crayons for this activity! Listen to the instructions and color the pictures to match what the teacher says. Then take turns saying out loud what color each classroom object is.

Nombre ______________________________

Yo practico

Your class is making a poster of classroom objects. Do you know what color each item should be? Listen to the commands. Circle the picture for each item and color the item.

1. Colorea la bandera en tu clase.

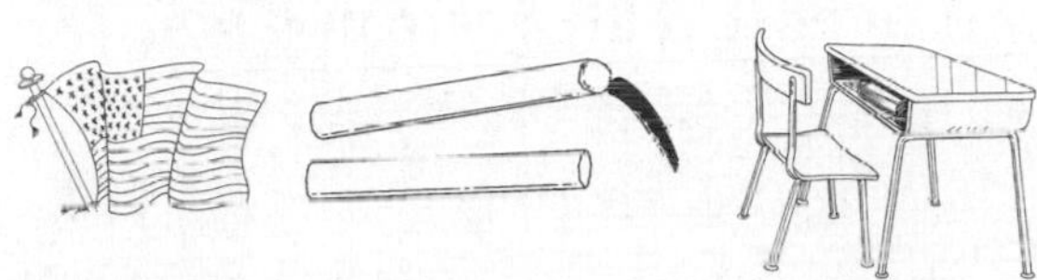

2. Colorea tu regla.

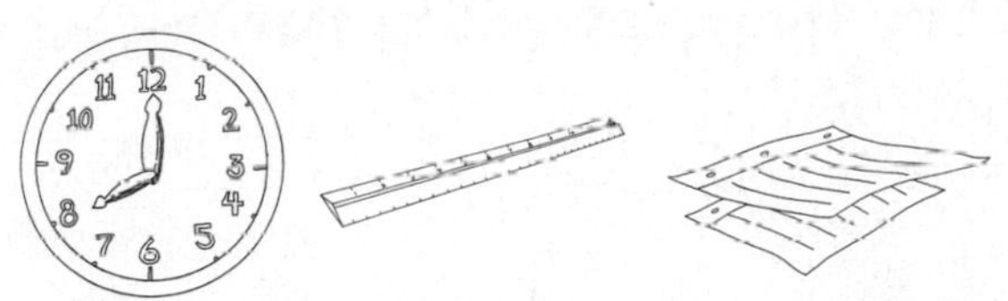

3. Colorea los libros en tu mesa.

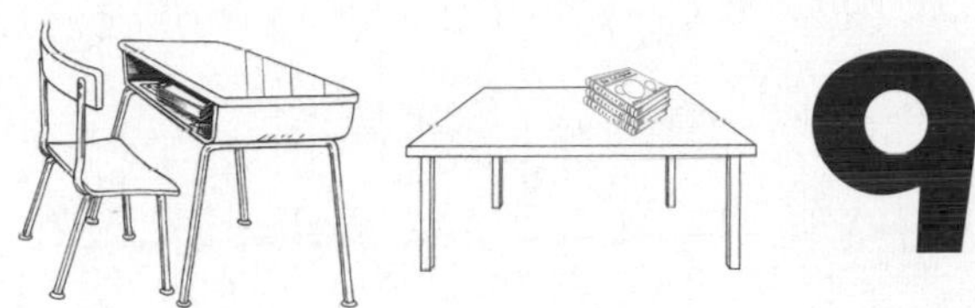

4. Colorea el pizarrón.

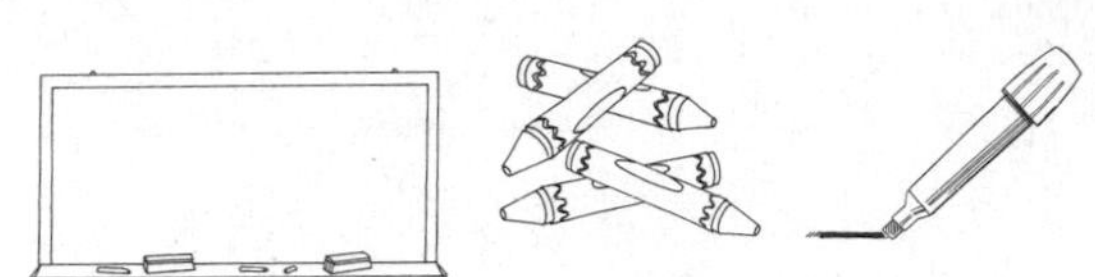

5. Colorea la tiza.

6. Colorea el escritorio del maestro.

7. Colorea los globos en tu clase.

8. ¿Qué color es tu color favorito? Colorea el color.

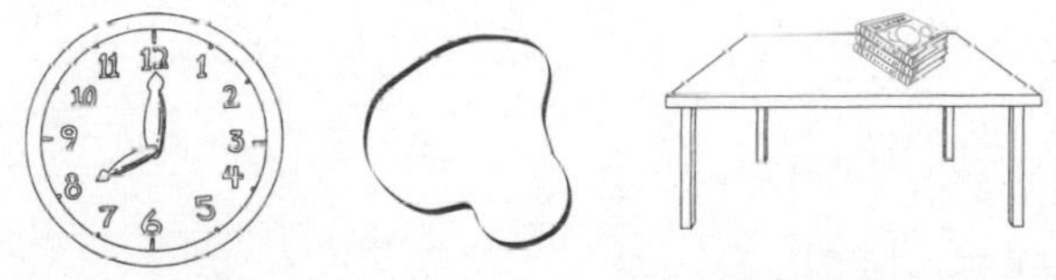

Nombre ______________________

Yo juego

To play this game, write a number between 0 and 10 on each bear and color each one a different color. You will need a small marker, such as a pebble, a bean, or a penny. Now you are ready to play the game! Place your colored picture on the floor and stand over it with your marker. Choose a bear and say the color and the number of the bear that you plan to hit. Then aim, and drop your marker. You earn two points if you name the color and number correctly, and three points if your marker lands and stays on the bear you picked. You may play with a partner. The first to reach eighteen points is the winner.

Nombre ______________________

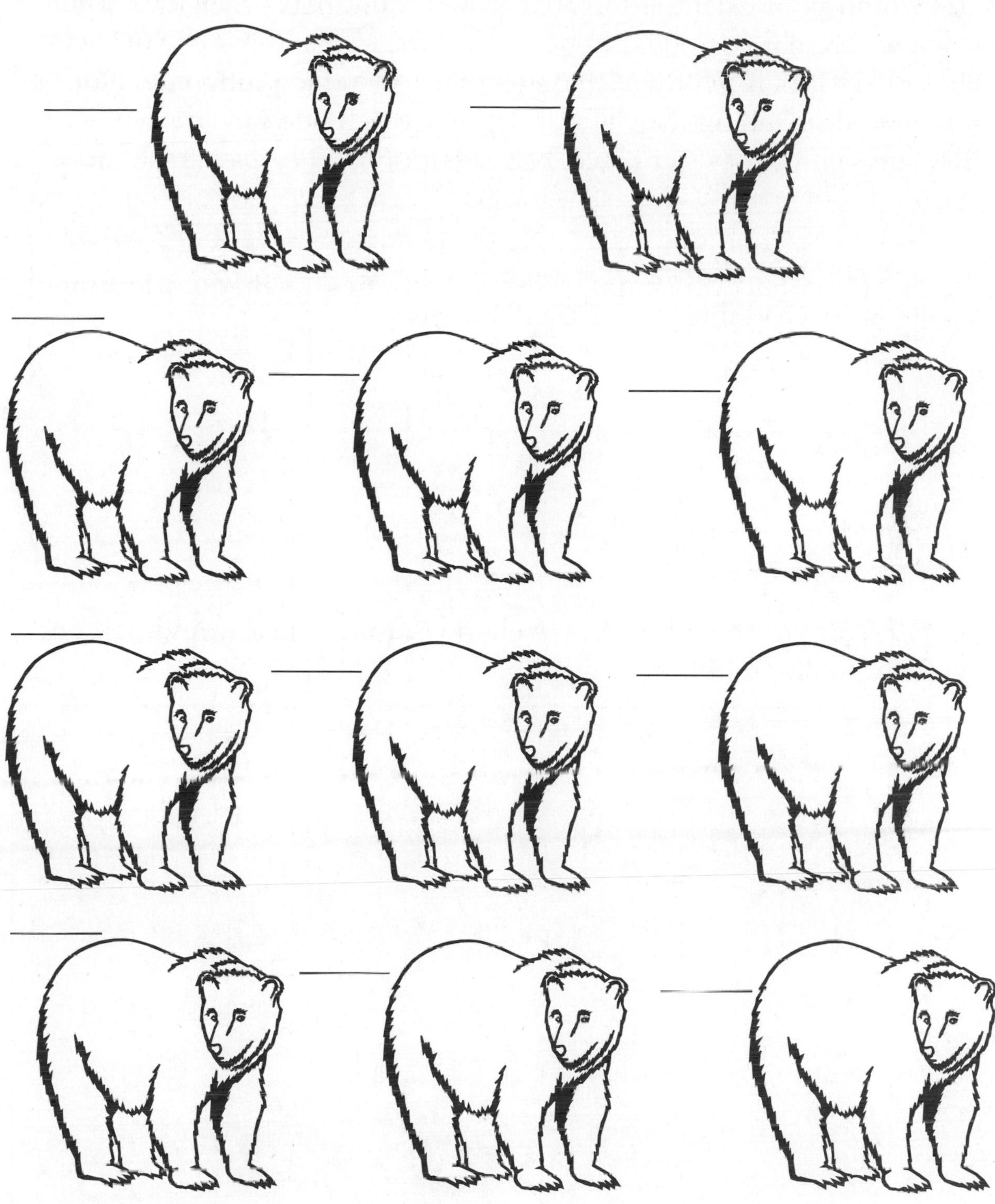

Nombre ______________________

Yo imagino

What would your calendar look like if you could make each day of the week a different color? Do different colors make you think of different feelings? Try it here. Color each day on this calendar a different color. Then take turns telling the class what color you made each day, and why. For example, **El lunes es blanco,** because Monday begins a fresh, new week.

lunes	martes	miércoles	jueves	viernes	sábado	domingo

Draw a picture to show how you feel on your favorite day and on your least favorite day in this box.

Nombre ______________________

Lección 5

Vamos a contar

Yo aprendo el vocabulario

once	11
doce	12
trece	13
catorce	14
quince	15
dieciséis	16
diecisiete	17
dieciocho	18
diecinueve	19
veinte	20

la figura

el cuadrado

el círculo

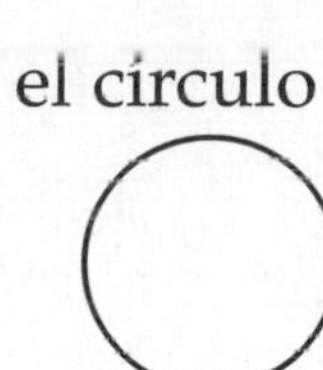

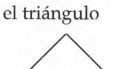

el rectángulo

el triángulo

el octágono

Más vocabulario

¿Qué número es?

Es el ____.

¿Qué figura es?

Es un ____.

¿De qué color es?

Es _____.

Nombre ______________________

Yo hablo

Your friend Juan just introduced you to his younger sister for the first time. Boy, does she ask a lot of questions! Listen to the questions. Then raise your hand and take turns answering them.

1. ¿Cómo te llamas?
2. ¿Cómo estás hoy?
3. ¿Qué día es hoy?
4. ¿Cuántos lápices hay en tu pupitre?
5. ¿Cuántas niñas hay en la clase?
6. ¿Cuántos niños hay en la clase?
7. ¿Cuántas sillas hay en tu casa?
8. ¿Cuántos relojes hay en tu casa?
9. ¿Qué figura es el reloj en tu clase?
10. ¿De qué color es el reloj en tu clase?
11. ¿Qué figura es el pizarrón en tu clase?
12. ¿De qué color es el pizarrón?

Nombre ______________________________

Yo practico

Congratulations! Your family just bought a little store. Your father made a list of things that must be put on the shelves. Listen to your father's list and draw the objects on the correct shelves. The first one has been done for you.

quince libros
cuatro calendarios
dieciocho computadoras
diecinueve reglas
ocho banderas
veinte lápices
siete globos
cinco marcadores
catorce creyones

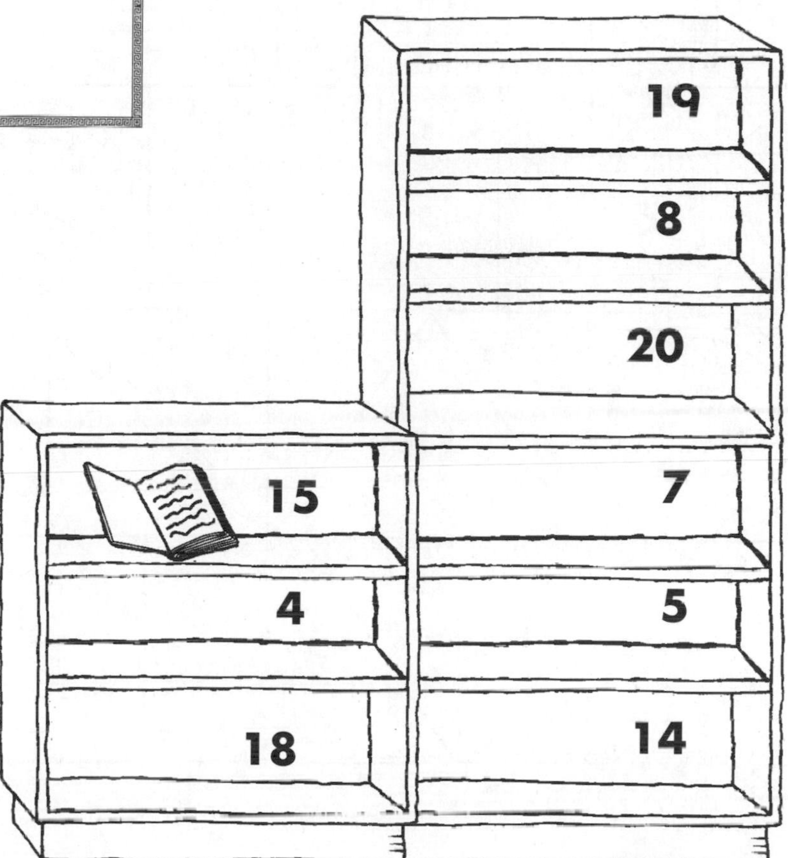

Nombre ______________________________

Yo juego

Your best friend is having a piñata party. In this game, move along the path, one space at a time, until you reach the piñata. If you land in a square, name the object that is in the square. If you land in a circle, say how that person is feeling. If you land in a rectangle, name the color of the fruit. If you land in a triangle, name the number.

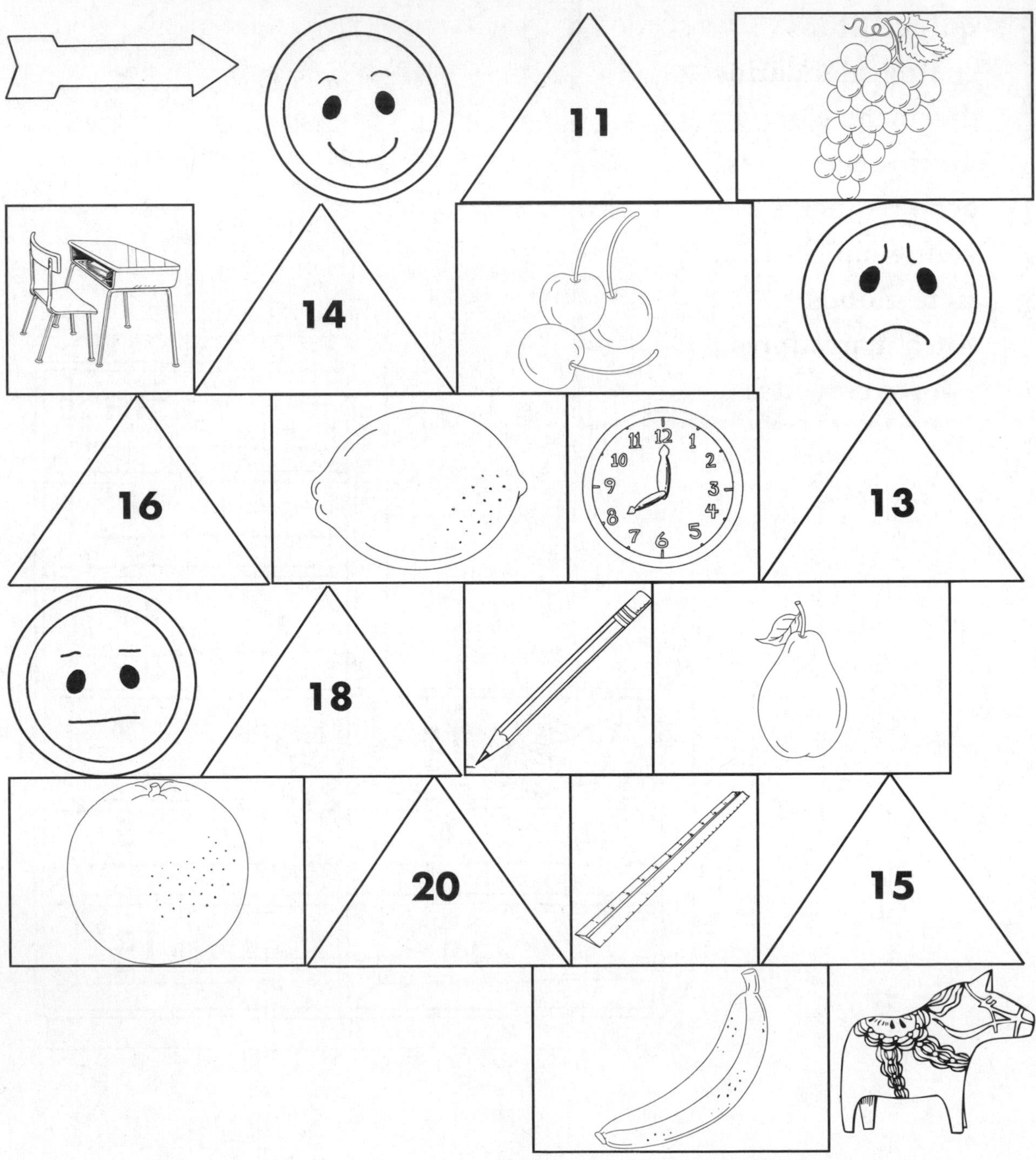

Nombre ____________________

Yo imagino

While deep-sea fishing, you find yourself surrounded by schools of the strangest fish! You count between 3 and 5 fish in each school. Each group has different colors and shapes! (There are circles, squares, rectangles, triangles, and even octagons!) Draw the schools of fish that surround you (at least four schools). Describe your fish for the rest of the class—remember to name your fish according to their color and shapes. For example: **triángulo rojo, círculo verde, octágono morado.**

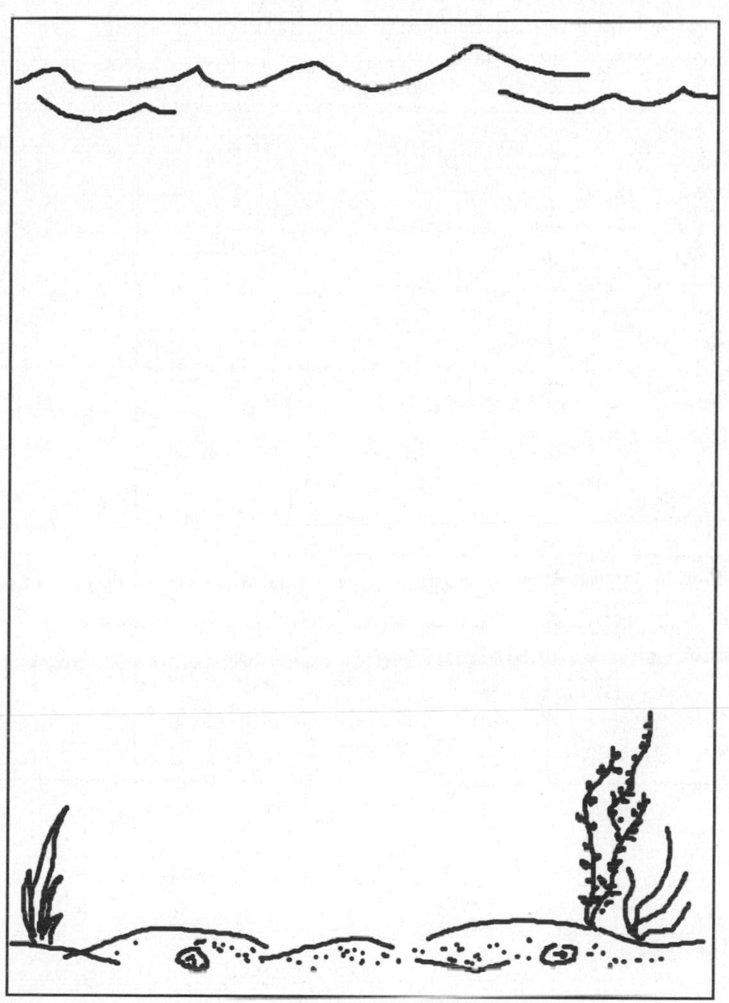

Nombre ______________________________

Lección 6

Vamos a aprender acerca de nosotros

Yo aprendo el vocabulario

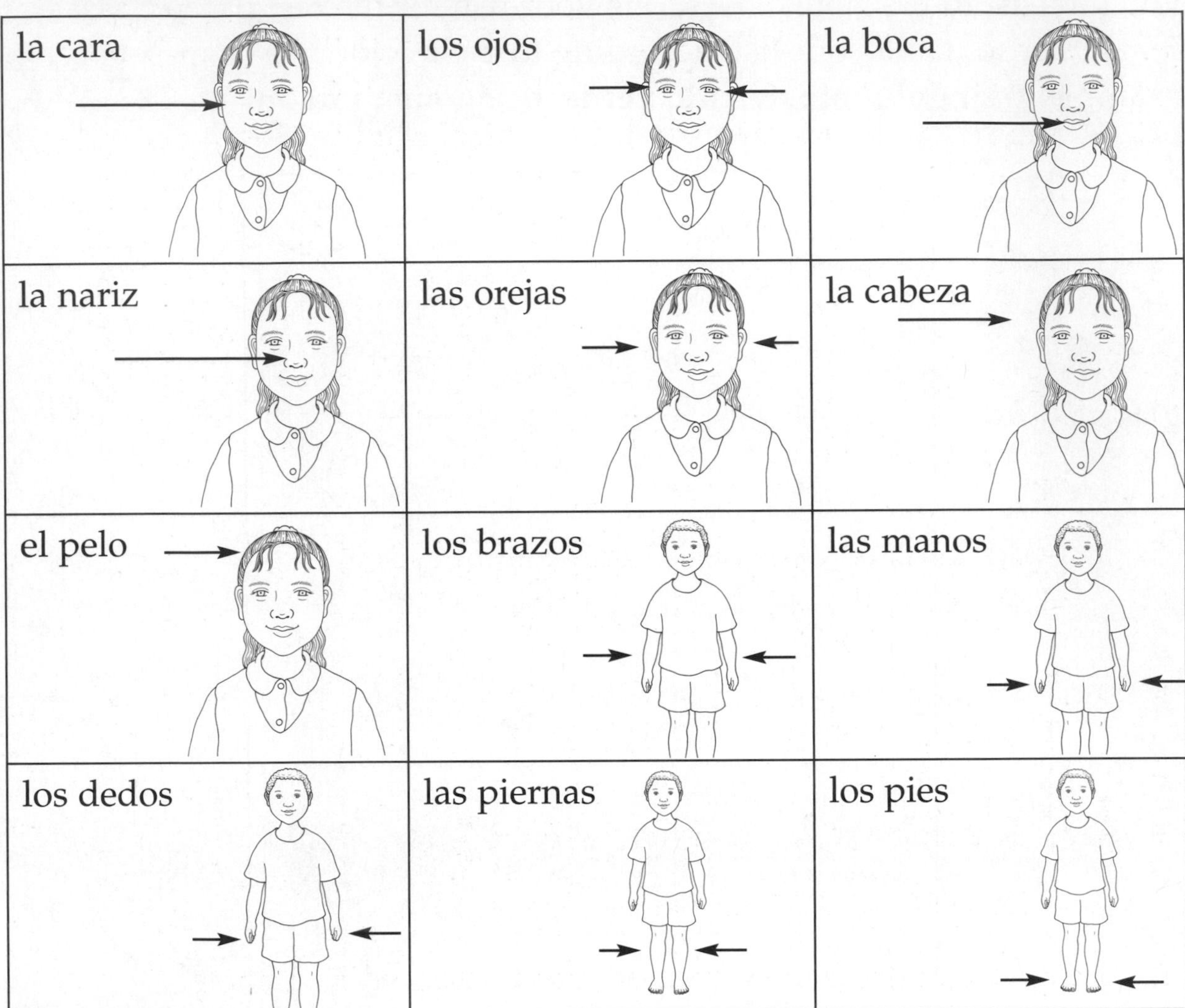

Más vocabulario

los

las

¿Qué es?

¿Qué son?

Son ____.

Nombre ______________________

Yo hablo

Your aunt from out of town is visiting your family. She wants to know all about your friends at school. Listen to her questions and watch out—some of them are silly. Then raise your hand and take turns answering them.

1. ¿Cómo se llama un niño con el pelo negro en tu clase?

2. ¿Cómo se llama una niña con los ojos azules en tu clase?

3. ¿Hay un niño con los ojos verdes en tu clase?

4. ¿Hay una niña con el pelo negro en tu clase?

5. ¿Hay una niña con las orejas verdes en tu clase?

6. ¿Hay un niño con los dedos rojos en tu clase?

7. ¿Hay una maestra con la cara azul en tu escuela?

8. ¿Hay un maestro con las manos anaranjadas en tu escuela?

Nombre ______________________________

Yo practico

Roberto is new in Spanish class and does not know the names for the parts of the body. Listen to Roberto's questions, then look at each picture and answer the questions.

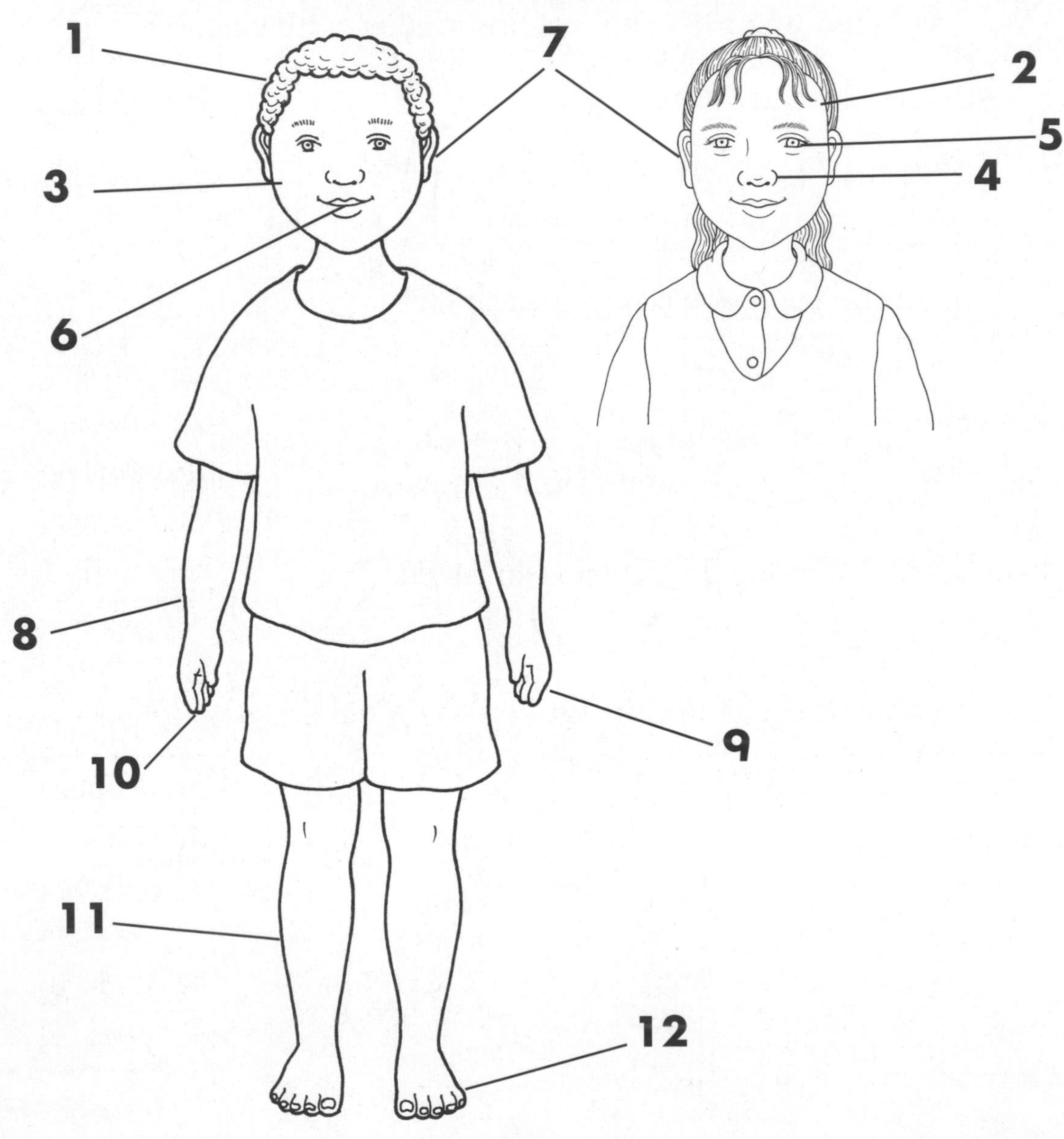

Nombre ______________________________

Yo juego

Imagine you are trying to tell your friends about a great monster movie you saw. Recall the phrases in each of the boxes. (The word **sin** in Spanish means "without.") Then draw a line from each set of phrases to the monster that it describes.

dos cabezas dos orejas dos brazos cuatro piernas dos bocas

una cabeza cinco ojos una nariz una pierna dos pies

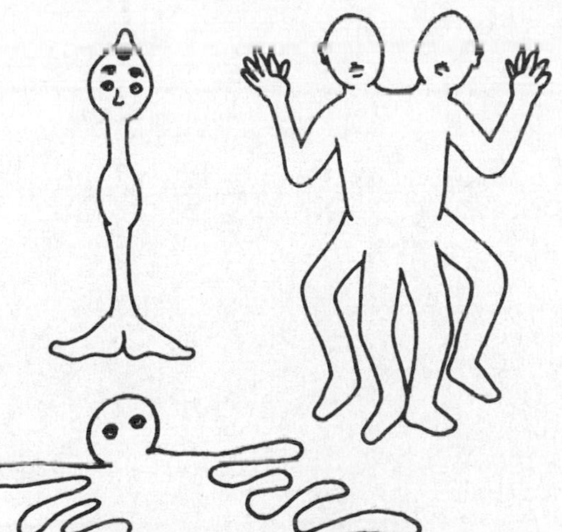

una cabeza cuatro orejas ocho manos dos pies sin pelo

sin cabeza sin orejas una boca dos brazos viente dedos

sin cara mucho pelo dos brazos doce dedos dos piernas y pies

una cabeza dos ojos dieciséis piernas sin brazos sin pies

Nombre ____________________

Yo imagino

Imagine you are trying to make a monster movie. You want it to be really scary! Draw a picture of the scariest monster you can think of. Label your monster's body parts in Spanish. Say what color the body parts are and how many your monster has. Then describe your monster to the class.

Nombre ______________________________

Lección 7

¿Qué animal es?

Yo aprendo el vocabulario

Más vocabulario

bonito
feo
grande
mediano/a
pequeño

¿Quién tiene ____?
Yo tengo _____.
¿Qué tiene ____?
El niño (Él) tiene ____.
La niña (Ella) tiene ____.

Nombre ______________________

Yo hablo

Your cousin has never been to a farm before, and is asking about some of the animals. Listen to the questions. Then take turns answering them.

1. ¿De qué colores son los caballos?
2. ¿De qué colores son las vacas?
3. ¿De qué colores son los cerdos?
4. ¿De qué colores son los perros?
5. ¿De qué colores son los gatos?
6. ¿Hay conejos morados?
7. ¿Hay gallos verdes?
8. ¿Hay gallinas grises?
9. ¿Hay pájaros azules?
10. ¿Tienes un perro o un gato? ¿Es grande, mediano o pequeño?
11. ¿Tienes un pájaro o un conejo? ¿Es bonito o es feo?
12. ¿Quién tiene un perro (un gato, un pájaro, un conejo)?

Nombre ______________________

Yo practico

Yesterday, children in señora Valdivia's class drew pictures of farm animals. Each child is holding his or her own pictures. Look at the pictures and answer the questions you hear.

Nombre ______________________________

Yo juego

How strange! You have just found a deserted farm. But wait! Some animals may be hiding here. It is up to you to draw the animals hiding on the farm. (You must remember their names and how many are hidden.) Choose a partner to find your hidden animals and to count how many of each there are.

Nombre ____________________

Yo imagino

Imagine that you are designing a brand new cartoon about farm animals. Color each of the animals below. Then take turns describing the animals to your classmates. Be sure to tell them what color they are. Which are pretty? Which are ugly? Which animal is small? Which one is big? Which one is medium? Ask your classmates too!

Nombre ______________________________

Lección 8

¿Cuántos años tienes?

Yo aprendo el vocabulario

Tengo frío.
Tengo calor.
Tengo hambre.
Tengo sed.
Tengo miedo.
Tengo sueño.
Tengo dolor.
Tengo prisa.
Tengo suerte.

Más vocabulario

¿Qué dice ___?
Dice «___».
¿Tienes ____?
Tengo ____.

¿Cuántos años tienes?
Tengo ___ años.
¿Cuántos años tiene?
Tiene ____ años.

Nombre ______________________

Yo hablo

Pretend that you are trying out for a school play. Listen to the following situations. Then take turns telling the class what you would say.

1. You only ate a banana for breakfast. Now it is three o'clock in the afternoon and you haven't had lunch yet. You say:
2. You are lying in bed on a dark stormy night and you hear a creaking sound outside your door. You say:
3. You are building a doghouse but you hammer your thumb instead of the nail. You say:
4. You step out of the bathtub on a chilly morning and realize your towel and robe are in your room. You say:
5. You just finished running a race, and your friend comes over with a bottle of water. You say:
6. You have been reading in your living room for a while and you have started sweating. You look around and you realize that the air conditioning is off and the windows are shut. You say:
7. It's Sunday morning. You have soccer practice at 10:00 A.M. It's 9:55 A.M. and you are still a few blocks away. You say:
8. Your older sister left behind in the bus the book she was reading on her way back home from school. She is nervous because the book is from her school's library and she may have lost it. Somebody finds the book and returns it to her. She says:
9. You were up so early this morning! You definitely feel like going to bed. You say:

Nombre ___________________________

Yo practico

It is Saturday morning. Call your friends to see how everyone is doing. Look at the pictures. Then raise your hand and take turns saying how each friend is doing.

1. Pedro

5. Bernardo

2. Alberto

6. Juan

3. Mario

7. Ofelia

4. Patricia

8. Elena

Nombre ______________________

Yo juego

How good a listener are you? Listen to the questions and answer them following these instructions:

- If the answer is a word or phrase, write it in the blank.
- If the answer is yes, find the picture that shows the answer and circle it.
- If the answer is no, find the picture that shows the answer and put an X on it.

1.

2.

3.

4.

5.

6.

7.

8.

9.

10.

Nombre ______________________

Yo imagino

Draw a group of your friends standing in line waiting to take the bus after school. Draw each child with a different expression, because each one has a different problem. What would they say if somebody asked them how they are doing? Take turns saying your sentences aloud. Don't forget to write the name of each of your friends next to his or her picture.

Nombre ______________________

Lección 9

Vamos a contar hasta treinta

Yo aprendo el vocabulario

veintiuno	21
veintidós	22
veintitrés	23
veinticuatro	24
veinticinco	25
veintiséis	26
veintisiete	27
veintiocho	28
veintinueve	29
treinta	30

Más vocabulario

¿Qué fecha es hoy?

Hoy es el _____.

Hoy es el primero.

Nombre ____________________

Yo hablo

Pretend that you are taking a survey in math class. Listen to the questions. Then raise your hand and take turns answering them.

1. ¿Cuántos niños y niñas hay en tu clase?
2. ¿Cuántos pupitres hay en tu clase?
3. ¿Cuántas mesas hay en tu clase?
4. ¿Cuántas reglas hay en tu clase?
5. ¿Cuántos lápices hay en tu clase?
6. ¿Cuántos maestros y maestras hay en tu escuela?
7. ¿Cuántos libros hay en tu casa?
8. Hay diez gatos. ¿Cuántos ojos hay?
9. Hay quince perros. ¿Cuántas orejas hay?
10. Hay doce niños. ¿Cuántas manos hay?
11. ¿Cuántos días hay en dos semanas?
12. ¿Cuántos días hay en cuatro semanas?

Nombre ______________________

Yo practico

Look at the happy group in the calendar below. Everyone will celebrate a birthday this month! How old will each person be? Listen to the questions and answer them.

Now decorate your calendar! Listen to the instructions and color the spaces in the calendar.

Nombre ______________________________

Yo juego

Señor Casares has a toy store. He just received a whole container full of new stuffed animals. Each animal has a tag with a number to help señor Casares remember how many of each animal he ordered. But the tags have gotten all tangled up! Follow the line from each animal to its tag. Then take turns saying which number goes with each animal.

Nombre ___________________________

Yo imagino

Imagine that you won one million dollars and decided to build a ranch for children to visit. You just bought the animals that will live on your ranch. In the space below, draw a picture of yourself with your animals. Draw each animal only once. Then, write a number between **uno** and **treinta** next to each animal, to indicate how many of each you bought. Finally, take turns describing your ranch.

Nombre ______________________

Lección 10

Vamos a aprender acerca de nuestra familia

Yo aprendo el vocabulario

la hermanastra

Más vocabulario

mi	alto	¿Quién es?
tu	bajo	Es ___.

Nombre ____________________

Yo hablo

You have made a new friend at school. His name is Esteban and he wants to know about your family. Listen to Esteban's questions. Then take turns with your classmates answering the questions.

1. ¿Cómo se llama tu mamá?
2. ¿Cómo se llama tu papá?
3. ¿De qué color es el pelo de tu papá?
4. ¿De qué color es el pelo de tu mamá?
5. ¿Tu papá es alto?
6. ¿Tu mamá es alta?
7. ¿Cómo se llama tu hermano?
8. ¿Cómo se llama tu hermana?
9. ¿Cuántos hijos tiene tu mamá?
10. ¿Cuántas personas hay en tu familia?
11. ¿Tienes un hermanastro?
12. ¿Tienes una hermanastra?

Nombre ______________________

Yo practico

A. Esteban also has some questions about your friends the Garzas. Look at the picture and listen to his questions. Then take turns answering the questions.

1. ¿Cómo se llama la mamá?
2. ¿Cómo se llama el hijo?
3. ¿Cómo se llama la abuela?
4. ¿Cómo se llama la hermana?

B. Listen to the sentences below and color the picture. Then take turns naming the hair color of each member of the Garza family.

1. Colorea el pelo de la mamá de rojo.
2. Colorea el pelo del papá de negro.
3. Colorea el pelo de la abuela de gris.
4. Colorea el pelo del abuelo de blanco.
5. Colorea el pelo de la hija de amarillo.
6. Colorea el pelo del hijo de negro.

Nombre ___________________________

Yo juego

Oh my! There was such a crowd at the county fair that many people got separated from their families or animals. Can you get everyone together again? Listen to what the people on the left are saying. Then draw a line from each person to the missing person or animal on the right.

Nombre ______________________

Yo imagino

Use the entire page to draw a picture of your family. Then color your picture. Finally, share your picture with your class and describe your family. Good luck!

Nombre ____________________

Lección 11

¿Qué tiempo hace?

Yo aprendo el vocabulario

Hace sol.
Hace frío.
Hace calor.
Hace buen tiempo.
Hace mal tiempo.
Hace viento.

Más vocabulario

¿Qué tiempo hace?

Hace ____.

Nombre ______________________________

Yo hablo

Look out the window right now. Then listen to the questions and answer them.

1. ¿Qué tiempo hace hoy?
2. ¿Hace sol?
3. ¿Hace frío?
4. ¿Hace calor?
5. ¿Hace buen tiempo?
6. ¿Hace mal tiempo?
7. ¿Hace viento?

Nombre ______________________

Yo practico

Pretend that your class is doing a weather report for a local television station. Draw a picture of your school in good weather, and bad weather. Next, describe the weather in each picture, and tell how you feel in each.

Hace buen tiempo.

Hace mal tiempo.

Nombre ______________________

Yo juego

Help Silvana get home. You have to follow these directions:

- If a space shows the weather, say in Spanish what the weather is and how it makes Silvana feel.
- If a space has a tree in the shape of a number, say that number in Spanish.

Nombre ______________________

Yo imagino

In the boxes below, draw four different kinds of weather. Then take turns describing your drawings to the class.

Nombre ______________________

Lección 12

Vamos a practicar lo que hemos aprendido

Yo practico

A. Roberto has just moved into the house next door and he wants to be friends with you. He has many questions. Listen to his questions and take turns with your classmates answering them.

1. ¿Cómo te llamas?
2. ¿Cómo se llama tu papá? ¿Cómo es?
3. ¿Cómo se llama tu mamá? ¿Cómo es?
4. ¿Cómo se llama tu maestra(o)? ¿Cómo es?
5. ¿Cuántos años tienes?
6. ¿Tienes prisa?
7. ¿Qué tiempo hace?
8. ¿Qué día es hoy?
9. ¿Qué fecha es hoy?
10. ¿Tienes un perro? ¿Cómo es?

Nombre ______________________________

B. What's on television? Look at the pictures below and describe what you see on each channel.

Nombre ______________________

C. The teacher has asked you to help her furnish the classroom. Listen to the teacher's list of classroom objects and draw them in the classroom below. You will need colored pencils or crayons to do this. Then take turns describing how you furnished the classroom.

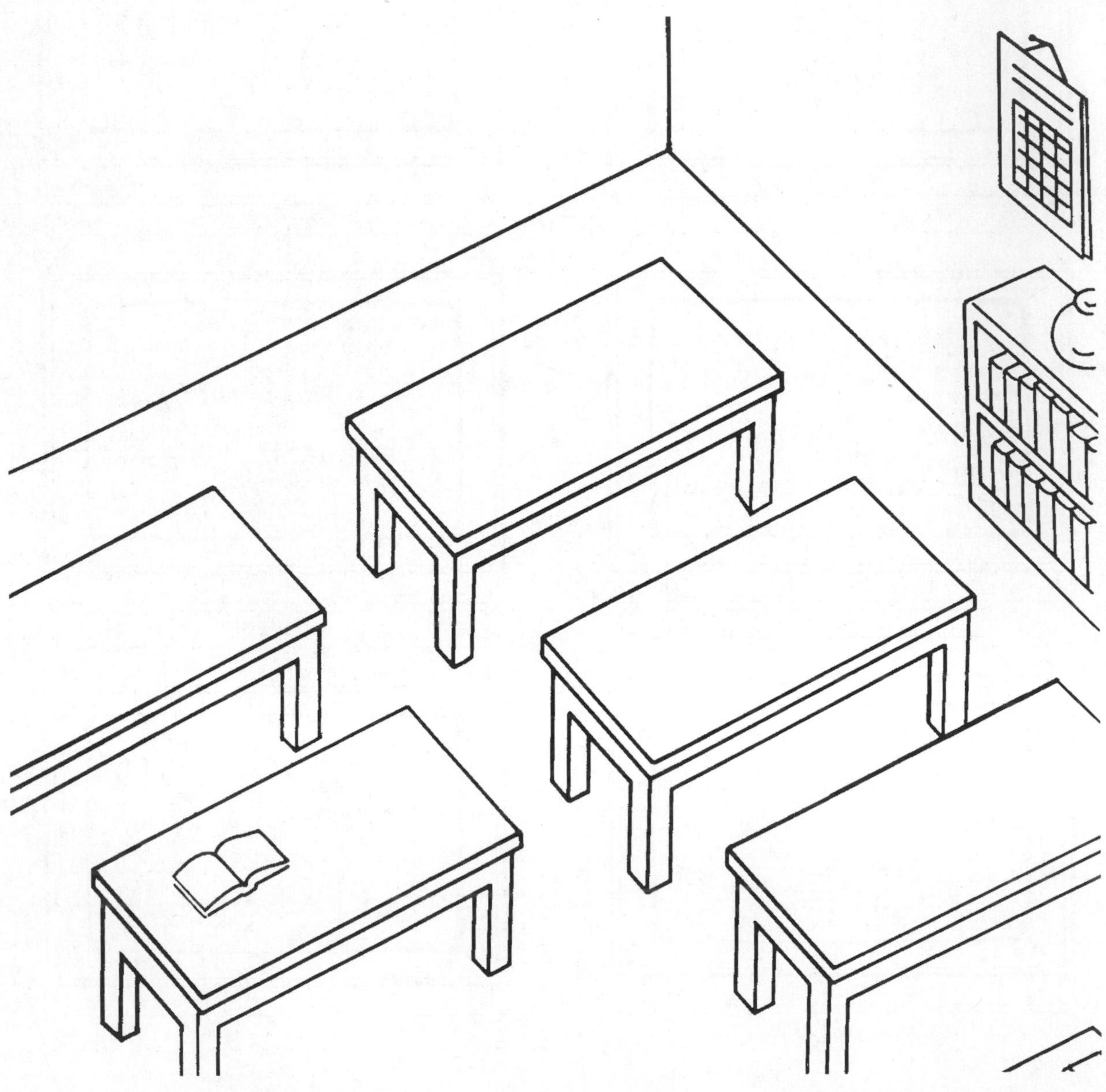

Nombre ____________________

Yo juego

Some of the farmer's animals escaped overnight, and are hiding. See if you can help the farmer find them, by connecting the dots below. Then raise your hand and take turns telling your classmates where you found each animal.

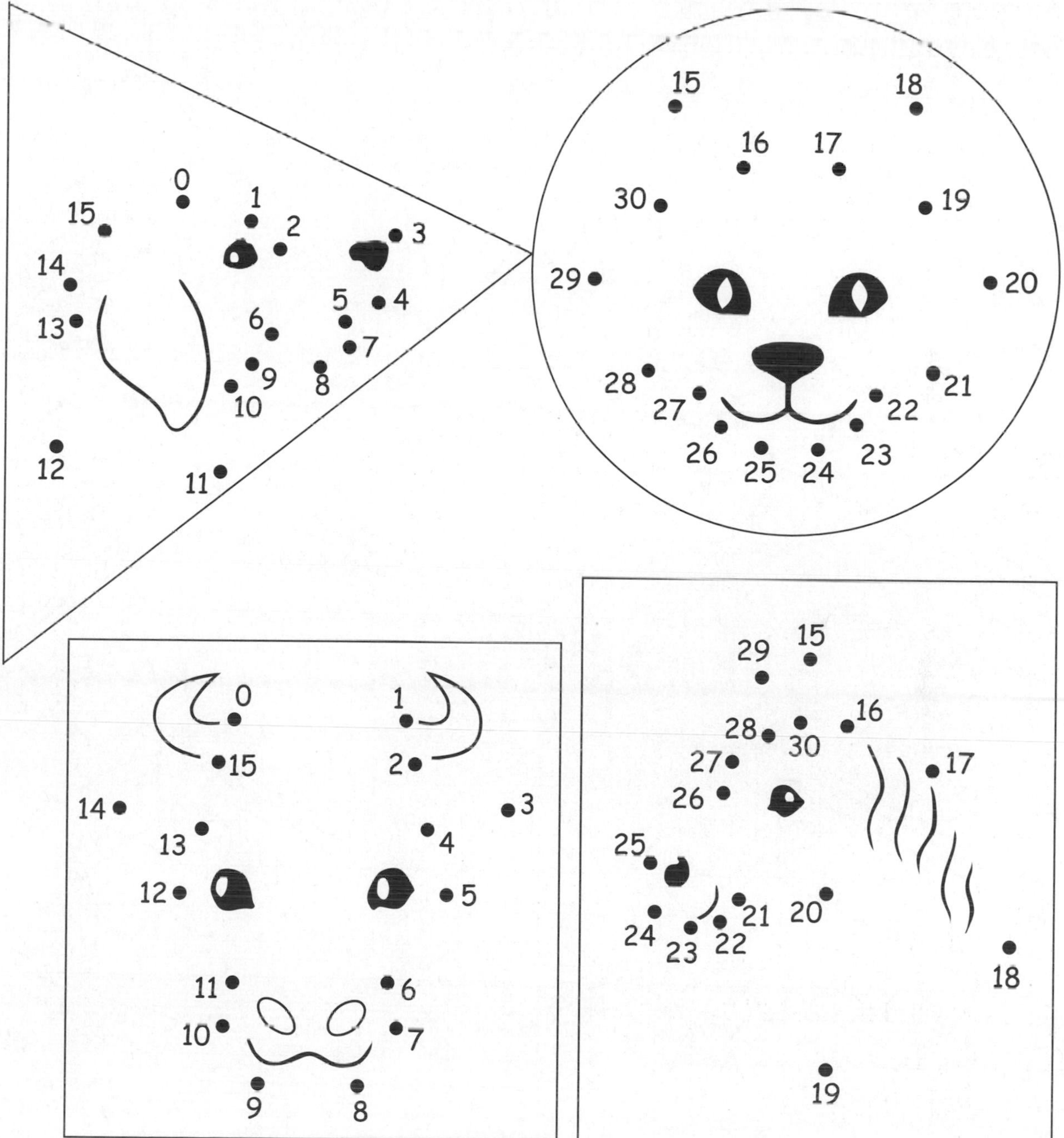

Nombre ______________________

Yo imagino

Sergio had a dream in which he won lots of money in the state lottery. In his dream, Sergio decided he was going to buy a farm and give each person in his family a different animal. He decided to name each animal after a day of the week! In the space below draw the different people in Sergio's family. Next to each of them draw the animal that you think Sergio would buy for them. Then describe your picture to the class.

Nombre ______________________

Lección 13

¿Qué mes es?

Yo aprendo el vocabulario

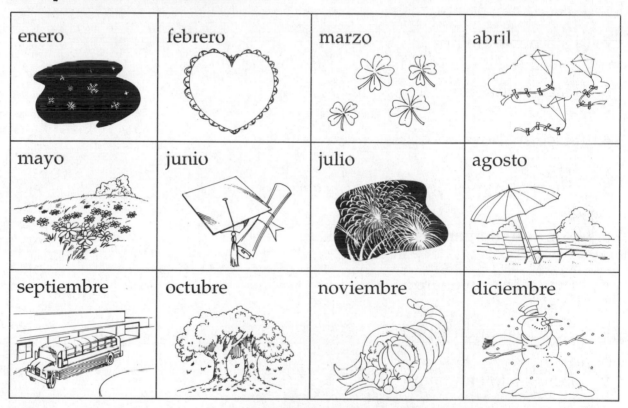

enero	febrero	marzo	abril
mayo	junio	julio	agosto
septiembre	octubre	noviembre	diciembre

Más vocabulario

el mes   los meses   el año

Está lloviendo.

Está nevando.

Nombre ______________________________

Yo hablo

You are in science class. Your teacher is talking about the weather. Listen to your teacher's questions and take turns answering them.

1. ¿Qué tiempo hace hoy?
2. ¿Está nevando hoy?
3. ¿Hace viento hoy?
4. ¿Hace sol hoy?
5. ¿Cuántos meses tiene el año?
6. ¿Cómo se llaman los meses del año?
7. ¿Tienes frío en enero?
8. ¿Tienes calor en febrero?
9. ¿Tienes frío en mayo?
10. ¿Tienes calor en agosto?

Nombre ______________________

Yo practico

A. Your new neighbor is from Argentina, where the seasons are the opposite of what they are in the United States. She wants to know what the weather is like each month where you live. Listen to her questions and answer them.

1. ¿Qué tiempo hace en enero?
2. ¿Qué tiempo hace en febrero?
3. ¿Qué tiempo hace en marzo?
4. ¿Qué tiempo hace en abril?
5. ¿Qué tiempo hace en mayo?
6. ¿Qué tiempo hace en junio?

B. What month does each picture remind you of? Take turns saying the names of each month out loud. Then color the pictures.

Nombre ______________________

Yo juego

You are a weather reporter at WRSK News (a Spanish-speaking radio station). Look at the map below and make up a weather report.

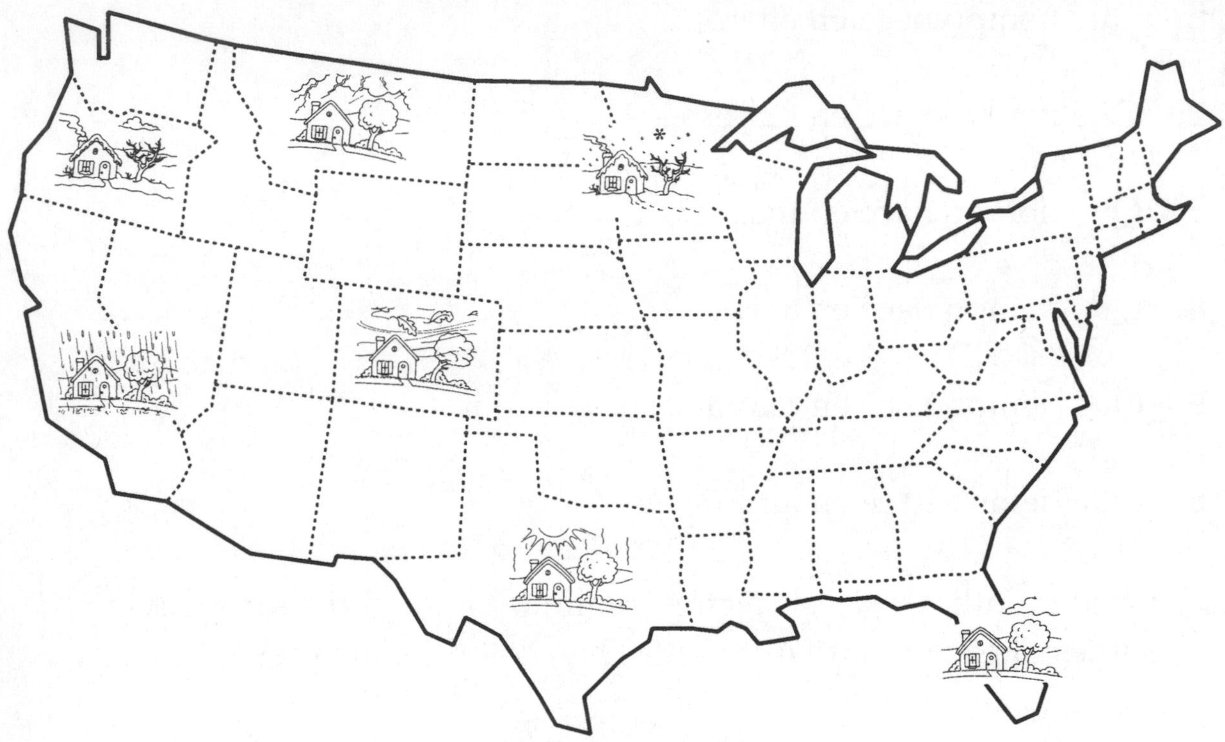

Nombre ______________________

Yo imagino

Below is a map of a fantasy land called "Fantasía." Give each "state" a name, and draw in rivers, lakes, and mountains wherever you want them to be. Then draw today's weather in Fantasía. Share your picture with your class and be sure to describe the weather in each "state." Tell the class what the weather in Fantasía is like in different months.

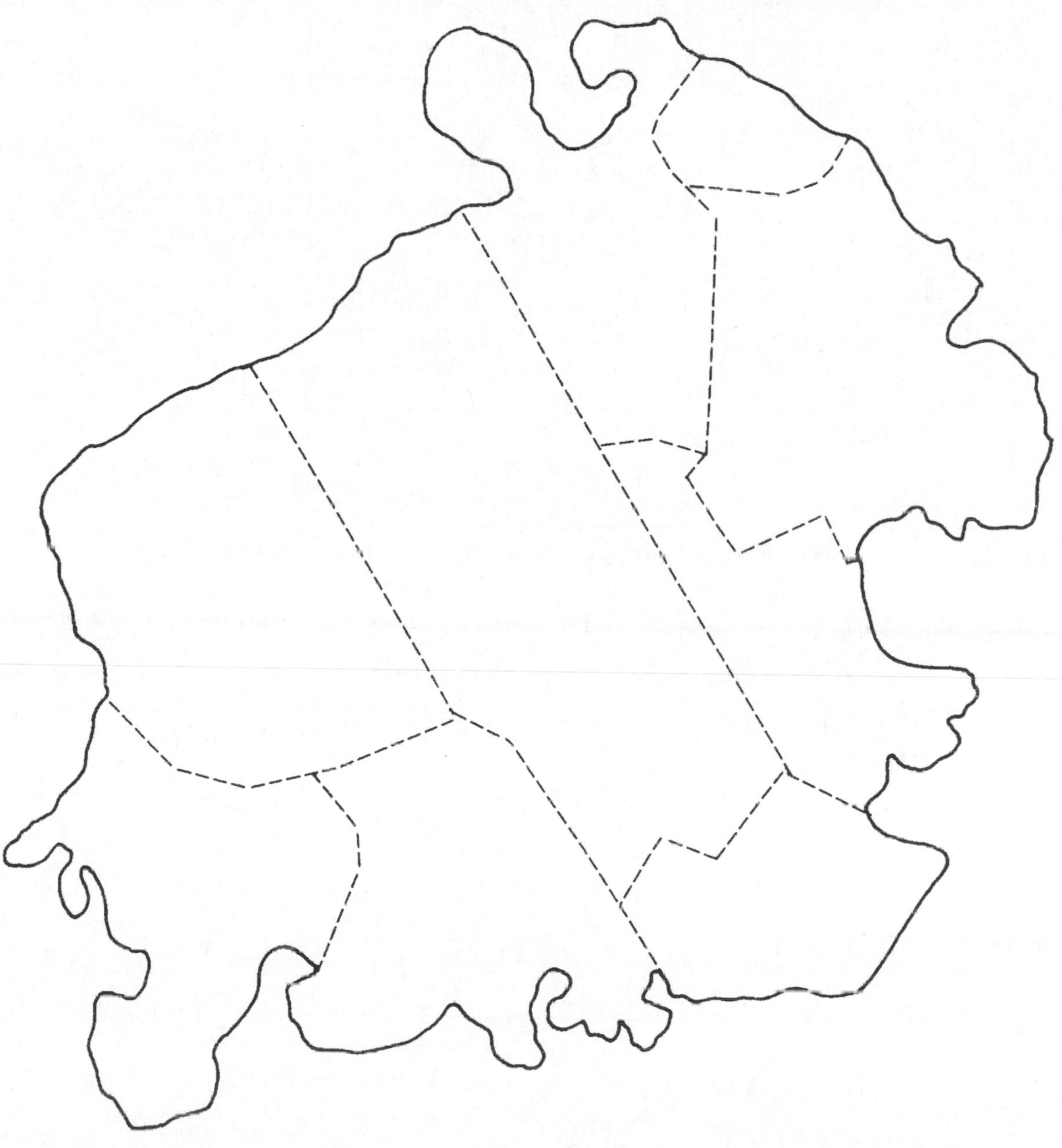

Nombre ______________________________

Lección 14

¿Qué llevas?

Yo aprendo el vocabulario

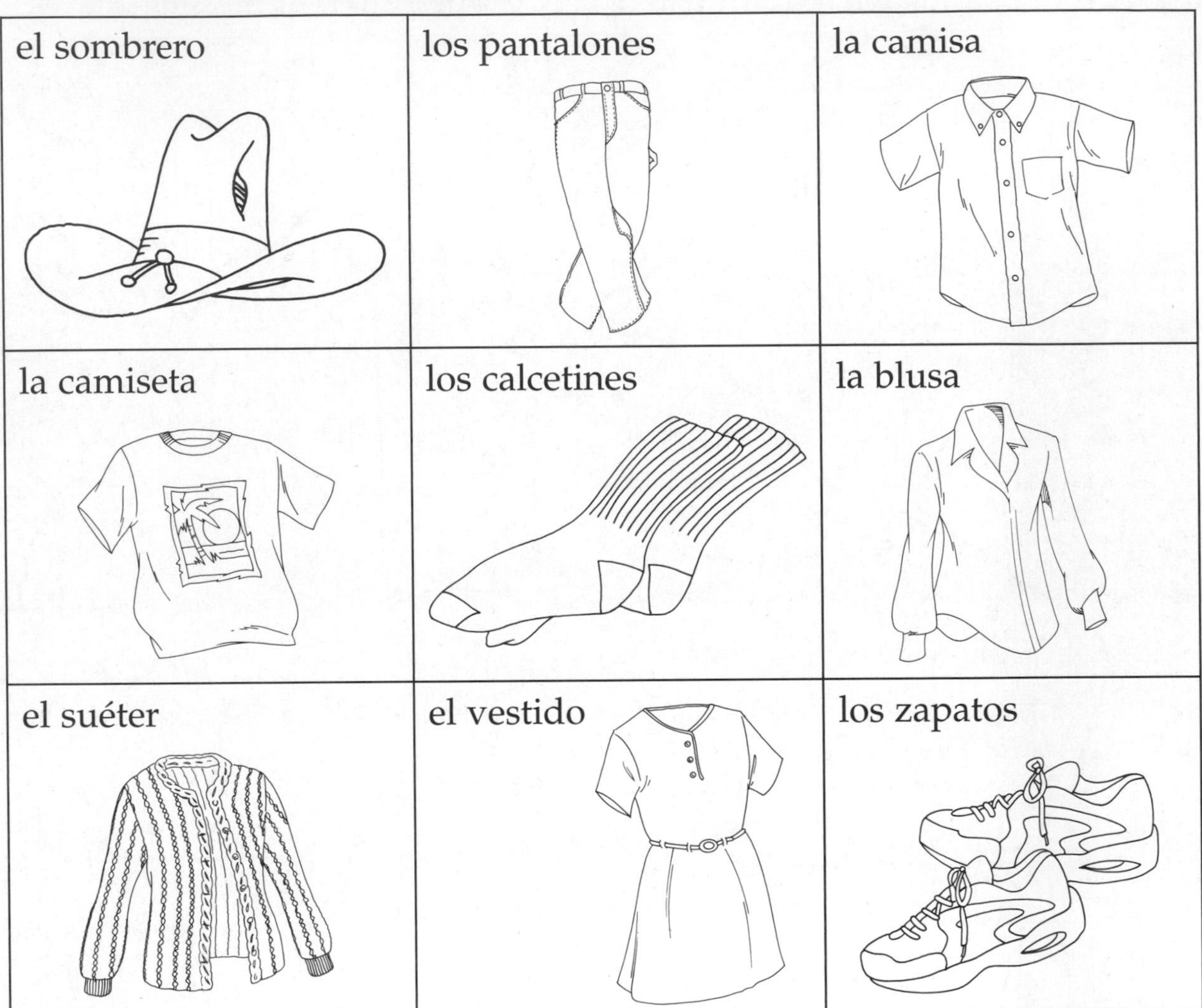

Más vocabulario

¿Qué llevas?

Llevo _____.

Llevo (un, una, unos, unas) ____.

Nombre ______________________________

Yo hablo

Your friend Margarita wants to be a fashion designer. She is always asking questions about clothing. Listen to some of Margarita's questions and take turns answering them.

1. ¿Qué llevas el lunes?
2. ¿Qué llevas el domingo?
3. ¿Qué llevas en enero?
4. ¿Qué llevas en marzo?
5. ¿Qué llevas en agosto?
6. ¿De qué color son tus zapatos favoritos?
7. ¿De qué color son tus calcetines favoritos?
8. ¿De qué color es tu suéter favorito?
9. ¿Cuántos suéteres tienes?
10. ¿Cuántos vestidos tienes?

Nombre ______________________________

Yo practico

A. Do you like colorful clothing? Color the pictures on page 68. Then take turns sharing with the rest of the class what color each piece of clothing is.

B. Señor Galván loves to dress up his farm animals for special days (although you might think they look pretty silly!). The animals think they look wonderful, and they prance around the barnyard, talking about what they are wearing. What are the animals saying today?

Nombre ______________________

Yo juego

Señor Ventura runs a successful toy store. His dolls are not selling well, though. Maybe if the dolls are dressed differently, they will sell better. Look at the pictures below and help señor Ventura dress up his dolls by drawing colorful clothing on them. Then, take turns describing the dolls' new clothes to the rest of the class. Don't forget to say what color each item of clothing is!

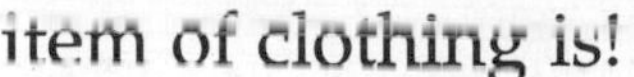

Nombre ______________________________

Yo imagino

Imagine that you are a famous painter. Everybody knows that you paint houses and landscapes beautifully, but few people know you are also talented at painting family portraits. It's time to show your talent! In the space below draw your family (including yourself) wearing each one's favorite clothes and shoes. Then color your picture. Finally, take turns showing your picture to the rest of the class and describing it.

Nombre ______________________

Lección 15

Vamos a contar hasta cuarenta

Yo aprendo el vocabulario

treinta y uno	31	treinta y seis	36
treinta y dos	32	treinta y siete	37
treinta y tres	33	treinta y ocho	38
treinta y cuatro	34	treinta y nueve	39
treinta y cinco	35	cuarenta	40

Nombre ______________________

Yo hablo

Your friend Margarita has questions about what everybody wears and when. Listen to Margarita's questions and take turns answering them.

1. ¿Qué llevas cuando hace sol?
2. ¿Qué llevas cuando hace viento?
3. ¿Cuántas chaquetas tienes?
4. ¿De qué color es tu chaqueta? ¿Es nueva?
5. ¿Qué llevas cuando hace calor?
6. ¿Cuántas camisetas tienes?
7. ¿De qué color es tu camiseta favorita?
8. ¿Tienes un traje de baño?
9. ¿De qué color es? ¿Es nuevo?
10. ¿Cuántos pijamas tienes?

Nombre ______________________

Yo practico

A. Marcos and Saúl are at the beach. How would they answer these questions: **1. ¿Cómo estás? 2. ¿Qué tiempo hace? 3. ¿Qué llevas?** Look at the pictures and take turns answering the questions for them.

B. Eloísa and Madgalena are on a snowy mountain. How would they answer these questions: **1. ¿Cómo estás? 2. ¿Qué tiempo hace? 3. ¿Qué llevas?**
Look at the pictures and take turns answering for them.

Nombre ______________________________

Yo juego

Señora Machado owns a dry cleaning store. She puts a tag with a number on each piece of clothing that she cleans, so she never gets customers' clothing mixed up. Now the tags have gotten all tangled up! Follow the line from each piece of clothing to its tag. Then tell señora Machado which number goes with each piece of clothing.

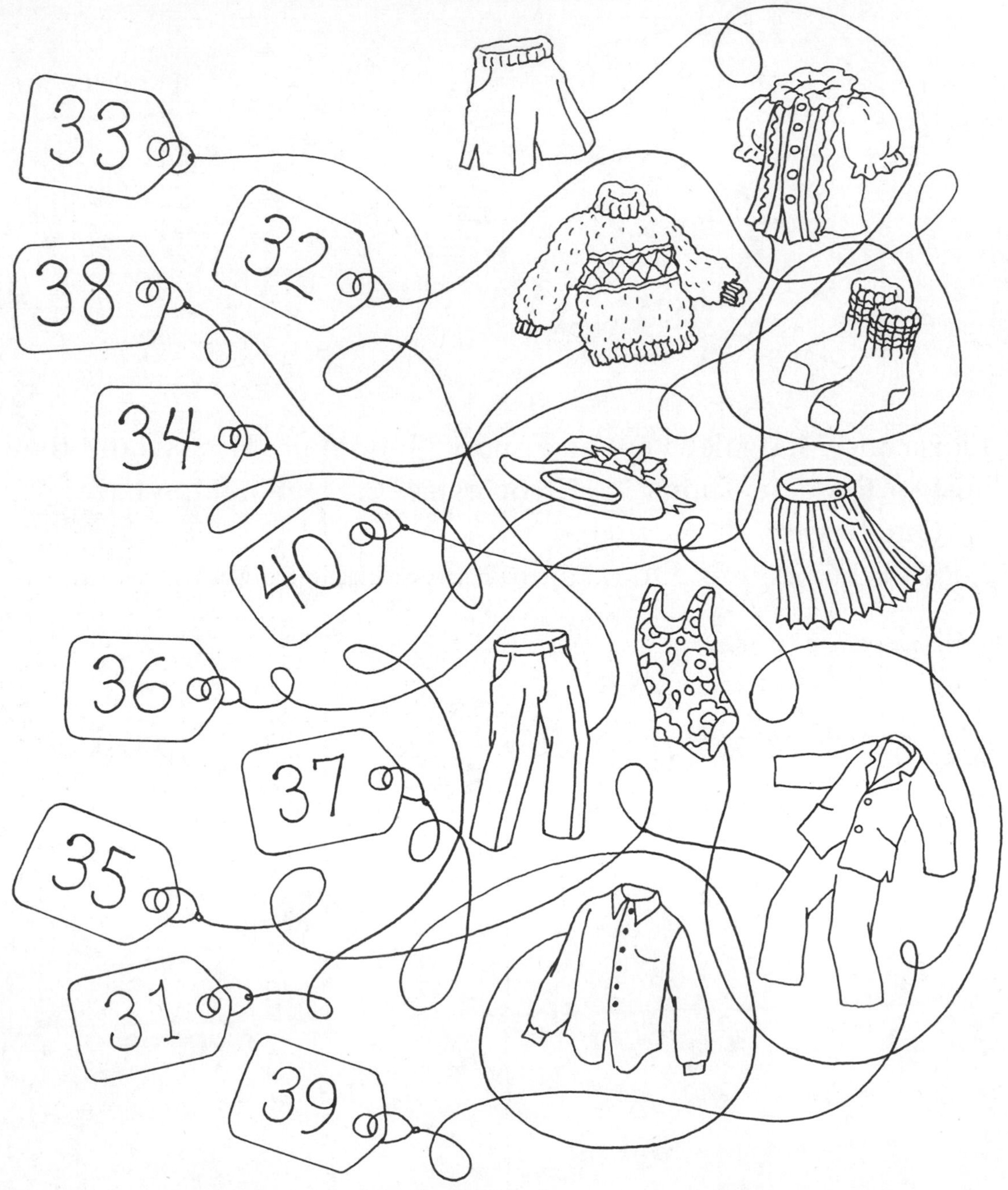

Nombre ______________________________

Yo imagino

How do you dress for each season? Look at each picture. Then draw a picture of yourself, wearing clothes that you would wear in that weather. Finally, take turns with your classmates describing your pictures. Describe the weather and the clothing in each picture.

Nombre ______________________

Lección 16

¿Cuándo es tu cumpleaños?

Yo aprendo el vocabulario

The sounds of the vowels **a, e**

Más vocabulario

su
mañana
¿Cuándo es tu cumpleaños?
Mi cumpleaños es el ___ de ___.
¿Cuántos (días, meses) / ¿Cuántas semanas hay en _______?
Hay ______.

Nombre ____________________

Yo hablo

A. You are buying birthday cards for your friends and family. The salesperson asks the dates of the different birthdays. Listen to her questions and take turns answering them.

1. ¿Cuándo es tu cumpleaños?
2. ¿Cuándo es el cumpleaños de tu mamá?
3. ¿Cuándo es el cumpleaños de tu hermano(a)?
4. ¿Cuándo es el cumpleaños de tu amigo(a)?
5. ¿Qué fecha es hoy?
6. ¿Qué fecha es mañana?

B. You are in math class. Your teacher wants to know if you can count days, weeks, and months. Listen to his or her questions and answer them.

1. ¿Cuántos días hay en una semana?
2. ¿Cuántos meses hay en un año?
3. ¿Cuántos días hay en dos semanas?
4. ¿Cuántos días hay en cuatro semanas?

Nombre ______________________________

Yo practico

You sure have a lot of friends! In the space below draw four of your friends (two boys and two girls). Then tell the class their names, how old they are, and their birthdays. Make your friends look good by dressing them up in colorful clothes!

Nombre ______________________

Yo juego

Toni has decorated this tree with ornaments for many special days of the year. Look at the picture and take turns saying the date of each special day out loud. If you are not sure of the exact day, make a guess or ask someone.

Es el 14 de febrero.

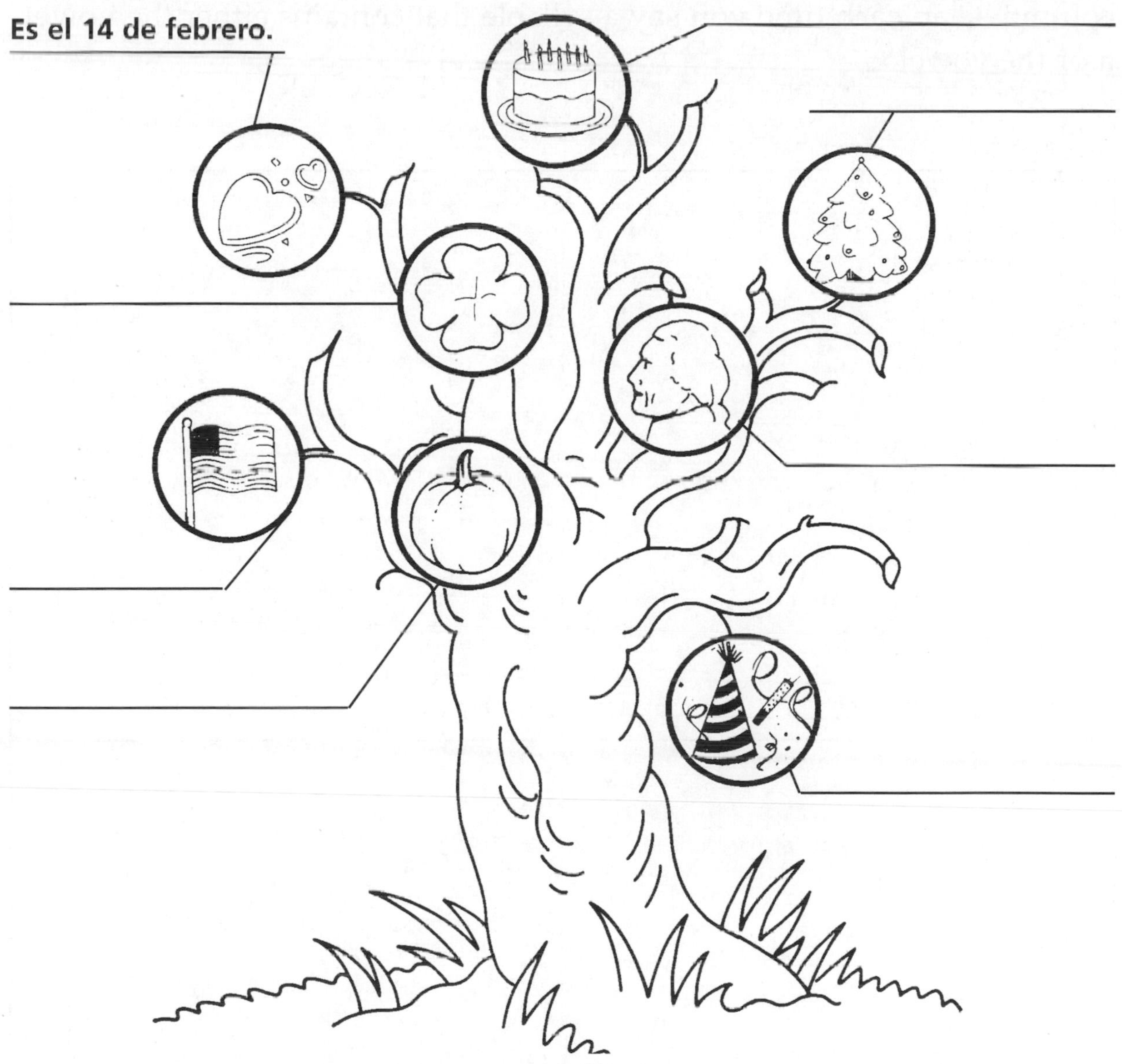

Nombre ______________________________

Yo imagino

In the top box, draw four items of clothing whose names in Spanish contain the vowel **a** but not the vowel **e.** In the bottom box, draw four classroom items whose names in Spanish contain the vowel **e** but not the vowel **a.** Then take turns saying the names of the items you drew in each column. Clap each time you say a syllable that contains either the vowel **a** or the vowel **e.**

Nombre ______________________

Lección 17

¿Qué hay en nuestra escuela?

Yo aprendo el vocabulario

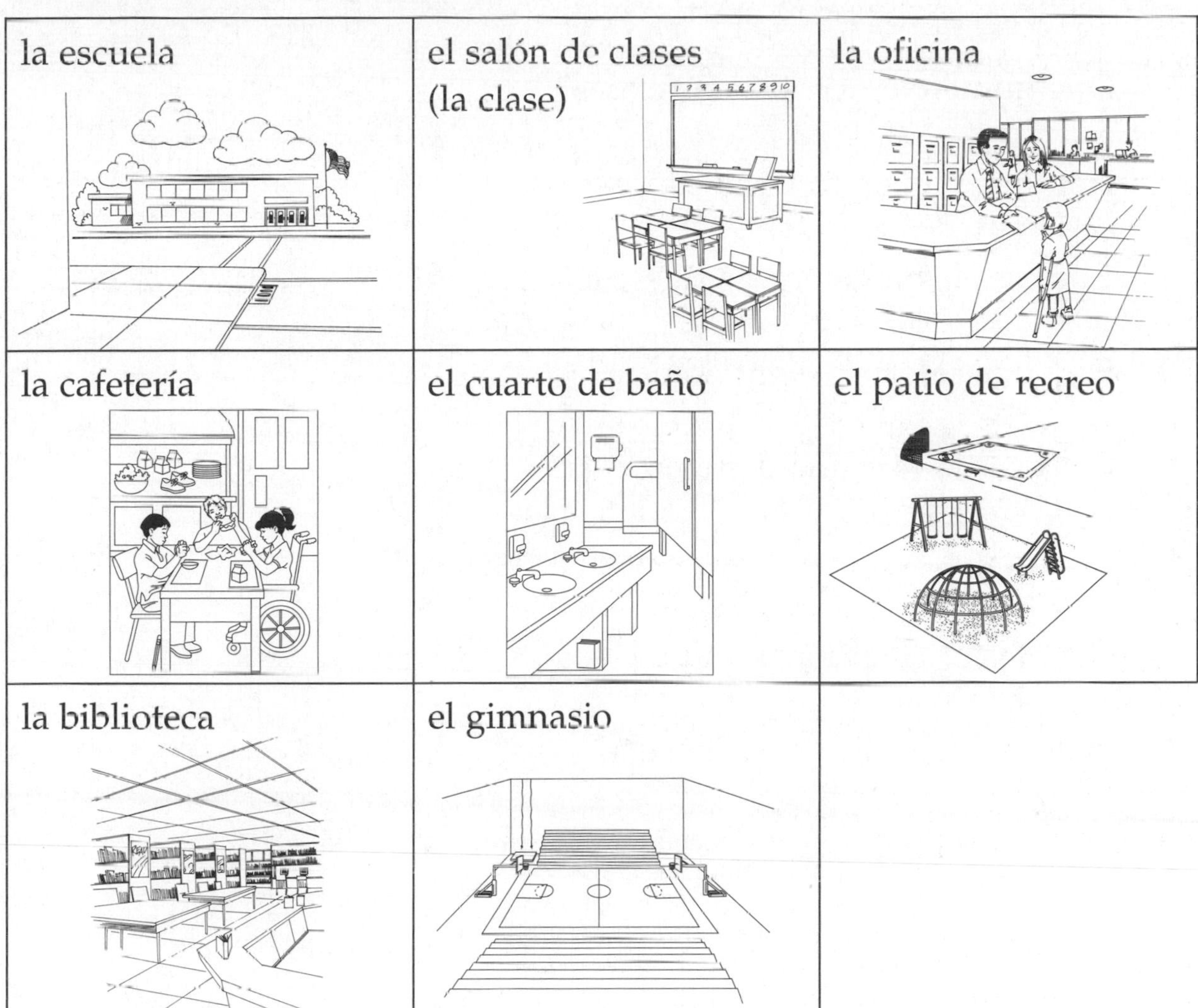

la escuela
el salón de clases
(la clase)
la oficina
la cafetería
el cuarto de baño
el patio de recreo
la biblioteca
el gimnasio

The sounds of the vowels **i, o**

Más vocabulario

¿Dónde está ____?

Está en _____.

¿Dónde están _____?

Están en _______.

¿Puedo ir?

Nombre ______________________

Yo hablo

Your neighbor, Diego, goes to a different school. He wants to know about your school. Listen to his questions and take turns answering them.

1. ¿Cómo se llama tu escuela?
2. ¿Qué número es tu salón de clases?
3. ¿Hay una biblioteca en tu escuela?
4. ¿Cómo es la biblioteca de tu escuela?
5. ¿Hay una cafetería en tu escuela?
6. ¿Cómo es la cafetería de tu escuela?
7. ¿Cuántos salones de clases hay en tu escuela?
8. ¿Cuántas oficinas hay en tu escuela?
9. ¿Hay un gimnasio en tu escuela?
10. ¿Cómo es el patio de recreo de tu escuela?

Nombre ______________________

Yo practico

Where in the school would you most likely find the following objects?

1. 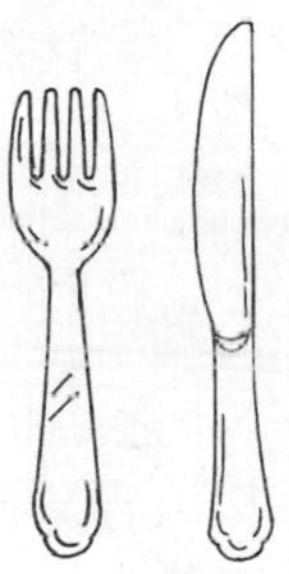

2. 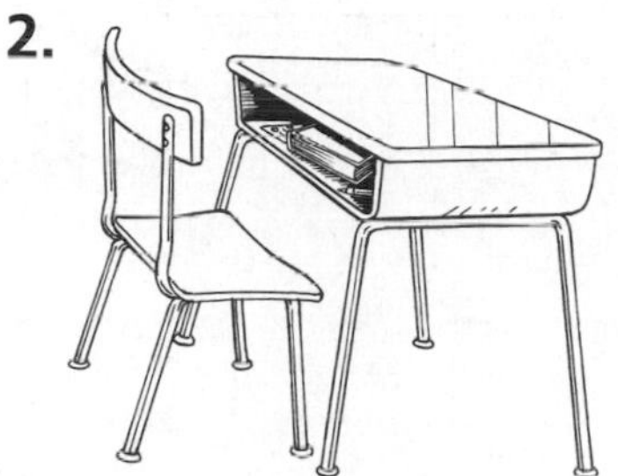

3. 

4. 

5. 

6. 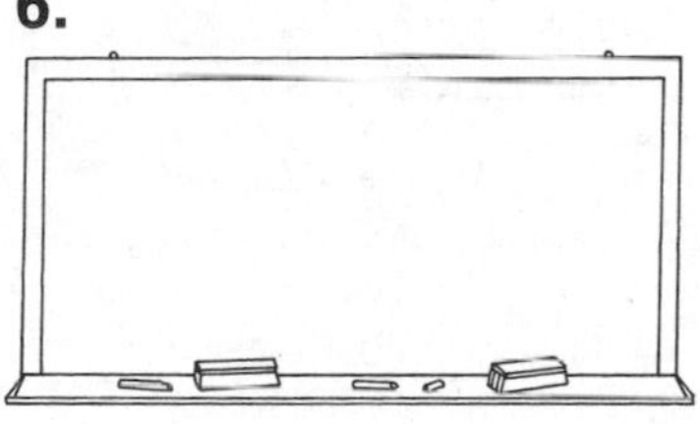

7. 

8. 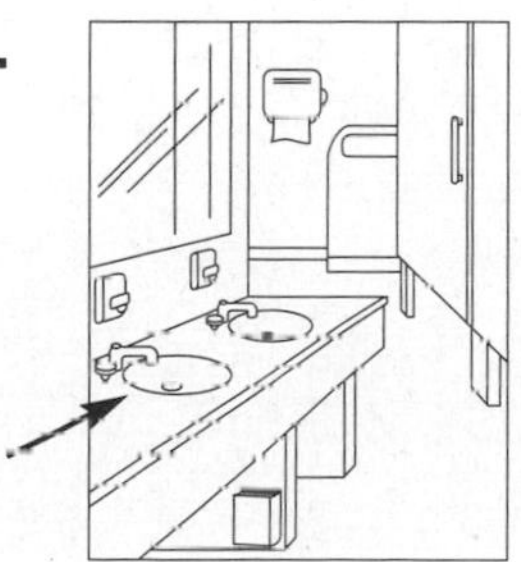

9. 

10. 

11. 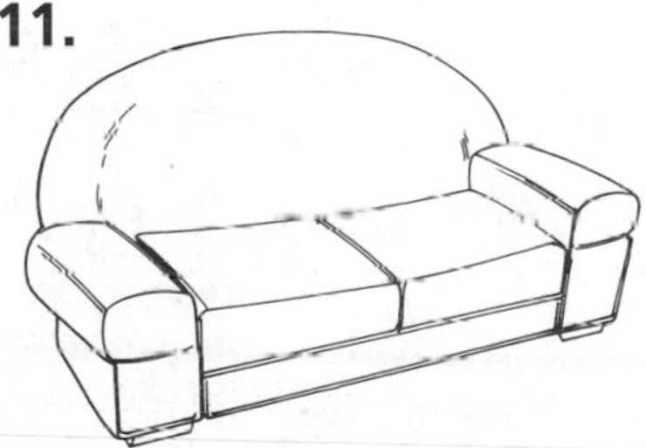

12. 

Nombre ______________________

Yo juego

There are twelve silly things in these pictures! Look at the pictures. Then find the things that do not belong in each one and circle them. Finally, take turns sharing your findings with the class.

Nombre ______________________________

Yo imagino

Draw a map of your school. Make sure you include some classrooms, the office, the cafeteria, a bathroom, the library, the gym, and the playground. Then draw three items of clothing whose names in Spanish contain the vowel **i** but not the vowel **o,** and three items of clothing whose names contain the vowel **o** but not the vowel **i.** Make each of these six things look "silly" by placing them where they do not belong. Take turns describing your map to the class.

Nombre ______________________________

Lección 18

Vamos a contar hasta cincuenta

Yo aprendo el vocabulario

cuarenta y uno	41
cuarenta y dos	42
cuarenta y tres	43
cuarenta y cuatro	44
cuarenta y cinco	45
cuarenta y seis	46
cuarenta y siete	47
cuarenta y ocho	48
cuarenta y nueve	49
cincuenta	50

rápido

despacio

The sound of the vowel **u**

Nombre ______________________

Yo hablo

A. Do you like math? Listen to the following math problems and take turns sharing with your class how you solved them.

1. Raúl tiene veinte perros y veinte gatos. ¿Cuántos animales tiene?

2. Lupe tiene cuarenta sombreros negros y ocho sombreros amarillos. ¿Cuántos sombreros tiene?

3. La maestra tiene treinta y dos lápices rojos y diez lápices verdes. ¿Cuántos lápices tiene?

4. El abuelo tiene veinticuatro calcetines blancos y veinte calcetines grises. ¿Cuántos calcetines tiene?

B. Let's watch the big race! Can you guess who will win? Who will come in second? Who will come in third? Who will come in last? After looking closely at the picture, take turns sharing your guesses with the rest of the class.

Nombre ______________________________

Yo practico

Why are some of the runners falling behind? Listen to some questions about the people you see at the race on page 89. Then take turns answering them.

1. ¿Quién tiene hambre?
2. ¿Quién tiene calor?
3. ¿Quién tiene sueño?
4. ¿Quién tiene dolor?
5. ¿Quién tiene sed?
6. ¿Quién está muy bien?
7. ¿Qué números tienen las niñas?
8. ¿Qué números tienen los niños?

Nombre ____________________

Yo juego

Now let's see YOU race! Say each number on the track aloud as quickly as you can. Go all the way around the track clockwise. Be sure to time yourself. You may race with a friend or by yourself.

Nombre ______________________

Yo imagino

Bird lovers from all over the world have brought their strangest birds to the Exotic Bird Show and Contest. Draw a different bird in each cage. Use many colors. Give each bird a number between 30 and 40. At the bottom of the page, judge your own birds by writing in the winning number in each category.

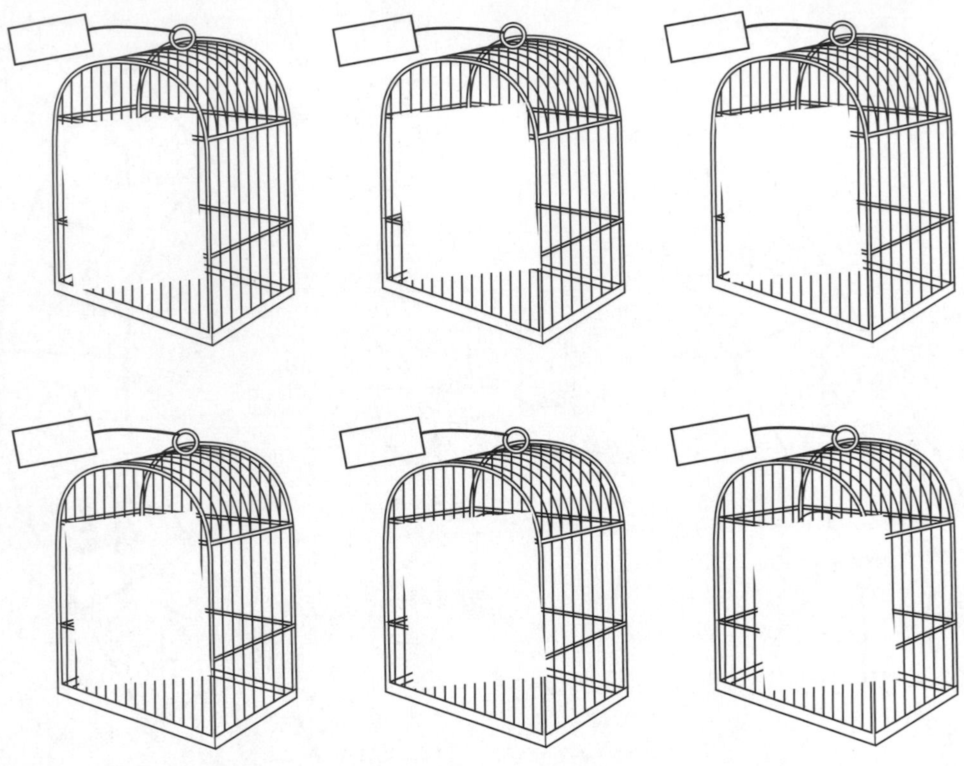

The prettiest bird is ______________________

The smallest bird is ______________________

The ugliest bird is ______________________

The most colorful bird is ______________________

The largest bird is ______________________

The funniest bird is ______________________

Nombre ______________________

Lección 19

Conocer a la gente de nuestra escuela

Yo aprendo el vocabulario

Nombre ________________________________

Yo hablo

How well do you know the people in your school? Take turns answering the questions.

1. ¿Cómo se llama el director (la directora) de tu escuela?

2. ¿Cómo se llama la enfermera (el enfermero) de tu escuela?

3. ¿Cómo se llama la secretaria (el secretario) de tu escuela?

4. ¿De qué color son los ojos de tu maestro (maestra)?

5. ¿De qué color es el pelo de la enfermera (del enfermero)?

Nombre ______________________

Yo practico

Mateo is curious about everything and he never stops asking questions. Look at the pictures and answer Mateo's questions about them. Then make up a few of your own questions for your classmates to answer.

1. ¿Dónde está la directora?

2. ¿Qué lleva el maestro?

3. ¿Cómo está Elena?

4. ¿Dónde está el enfermero?

5. ¿Quién es la secretaria?

6. ¿Cómo está la directora?

7. ¿Quién es el enfermero?

Nombre ______________________________

Yo juego

It has been a long week at Ibarra Elementary School. The clinic is very busy! But today is Friday, and everyone will soon have a weekend to get well. Listen to the story and draw a picture of the scene described in the story. Draw your picture on a separate piece of paper.

Cuatro personas están en la oficina de la enfermera de la escuela. El director está muy mal. La enfermera dice al director, "¿Qué tiene usted, señor Chávez?" El director dice, "Tengo mucho dolor de cabeza." La maestra está muy mal. La enfermera dice a la maestra, "¿Qué tiene usted, señorita Núñez?" La maestra dice, "Tengo mucho sueño." La secretaria está muy mal. La enfermera dice, "¿Qué tiene usted, señora López?" La secretaria dice, "Tengo mucho frío." Juan tiene seis años. Él está muy mal también. La enfermera dice, "¿Qué tienes, Juan?" Juan dice, "Tengo mucha hambre."

Nombre ______________________

Yo imagino

In the boxes below, draw some of the people in your school. Include the principal, the secretary, the nurse, some teachers, and a few of your classmates. Draw each person in the school room where they are usually found. Then color your pictures different colors. While you draw your picture, think of how each person feels and try to show that in your picture. Then take turns describing your picture to the class.

Nombre ______________________

Lección 20

¿Cómo estás hoy?

Yo aprendo el vocabulario

Estoy contento.
Estoy contenta.
Estoy triste.
Estoy enojado.
Estoy enojada.

Más vocabulario

¿Qué tal?

Nombre ____________________

Yo hablo

What would you say in the following situations? Take turns saying it to the class.

1. Your music teacher just told you that you have a beautiful voice! You say:

2. You just found out that your best friend is moving to another state. You say:

3. You finally finished your science project. It's a windmill made completely out of popsicle sticks, and it really works! Then your baby sister sits on it. You say:

4. Your father just sat on some chewing gum that you left in his favorite chair. He says:

5. Your sister won a radio contest and received free tickets to a sold-out concert. She says:

6. Your mother is sitting on the sofa, crying, while watching an old movie on TV. You ask her why she's crying. She says:

Nombre ______________________________

Yo practico

Paquita does not know the story of Goldilocks and the three bears. She wants to know what each character pictured below is saying. Look at the pictures and take turns telling Paquita what each character is saying.

Nombre ____________________

Yo juego

These two pictures may look the same, but there are eight differences. Find the differences on the bottom picture and circle them. Then take turns explaining the differences to the class.

13—Martín
28—Rosa
32—Felipe
45—Nicolás
47—Maruja
49—Lola
50—Pilar

Nombre ______________________________

Yo imagino

How do you feel at different times? Read the sentence over each box. Then draw your face in the box and write how you feel. The first one has been done for you.

Es el 4 de julio.

Estoy contenta.

Tengo calor.

Tengo sed.

Es el 31 de octubre.

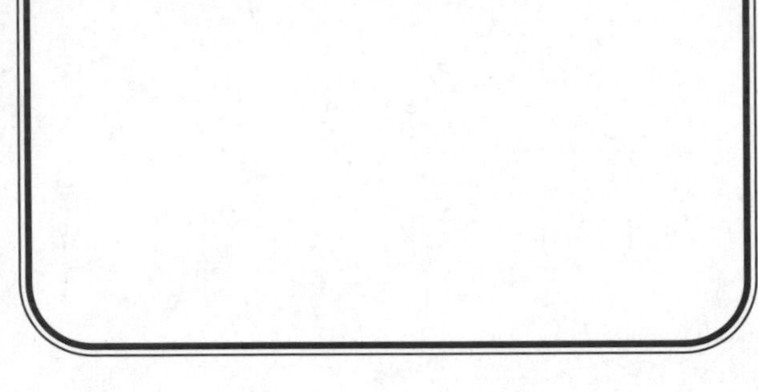

Es mi cumpleaños.

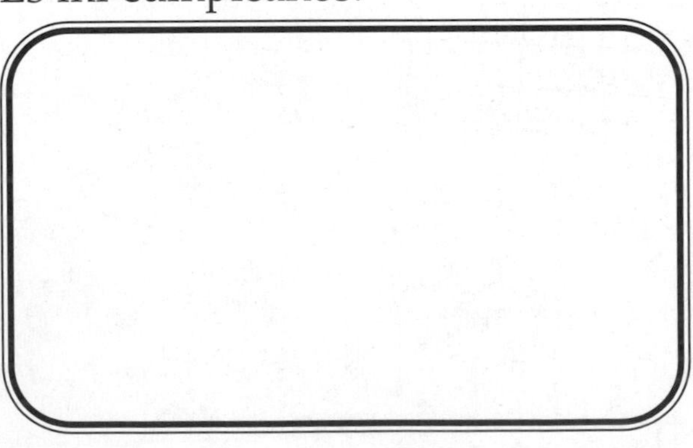

Mi hermano lleva mi camisa favorita.

Nombre ______________________________

Lección 21

Vamos a hablar por teléfono

Yo aprendo el vocabulario

el teléfono

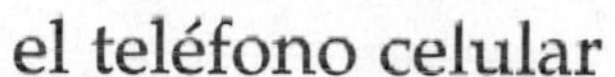
el teléfono celular

Más vocabulario

¿Qué haces?

Hablo por teléfono.

Marca el número _______.

Nombre ______________________

Yo hablo

Your older sister needs to take a survey on telephone use for her social studies class. She wants to practice asking first. Listen to her questions and answer them.

1. ¿Cómo te llamas?
2. ¿Cuántos años tienes?
3. ¿De qué color es el teléfono de tu casa?
4. ¿Es nuevo?
5. ¿Tienes un teléfono celular?
6. ¿Es nuevo?
7. ¿Hablas por teléfono con tus amigos?
8. ¿Hablas por teléfono con tu papá (mamá, abuelo, abuela)?
9. ¿Quién tiene un teléfono celular en tu familia?

Nombre ______________________

Yo practico

Are you good at remembering telephone numbers? See how many telephone numbers you can remember. You can include cellular telephone numbers. Write each telephone number on the note pad below. Next, take turns pretending to "dial" one of your six telephone numbers by touching the numbers on the phone below, while saying each number. **El número de teléfono es cinco, cinco, cinco** ________.

Nombre ___________________________

Yo juego

How do you feel at different times? Draw your face under each picture and take turns saying how you usually feel in each situation.

Nombre ______________________

Yo imagino

How much can you say about each of these pictures? Remember to talk about the weather, the people, how old they are, what they are wearing, what they are doing, and how they feel. It's all up to you! Take turns describing each picture to the class.

Nombre ______________________

Lección 22

Vamos a cruzar la calle

Yo aprendo el vocabulario

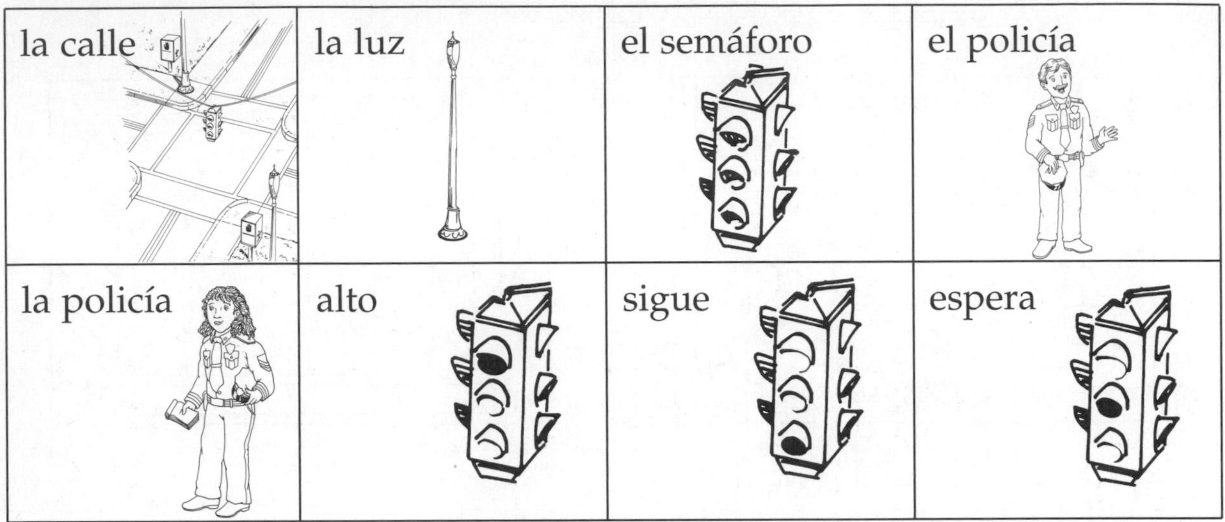

la calle	la luz	el semáforo	el policía
la policía	alto	sigue	espera

Más vocabulario

Miro a la derecha. Miro a la izquierda. Cruzo la calle.

Nombre ______________________

Yo hablo

A police officer visited class to talk about safety and traffic lights. She wants to know if the class understood everything she said. Listen to her questions and take turns answering them.

1. ¿Cuántas luces tiene el semáforo?
2. ¿De qué colores son las luces del semáforo?
3. ¿Qué dice la luz roja?
4. ¿Qué dice la luz amarilla?
5. ¿Qué dice la luz verde?
6. ¿Hay un semáforo en la calle de tu escuela?
7. ¿Hay un semáforo en la calle de tu casa?
8. ¿Qué lleva el policía o la policía?

Nombre ______________________________

Yo practico

This is a street corner in Ciudad Bonita. Look at the picture and name everything you can in Spanish. Then make up a sentence for each thing you named. For example, you might say **"Es la policía. La policía dice <<Sigue>>."**

Nombre ______________________

Yo juego

Although no one in the scene below is talking, they are all very busy with their thoughts. Can you read their minds? Take turns saying what you think each person is thinking.

Nombre ______________________

Yo imagino

If only you could see what interesting objects are at the bottom of muddy lakes! Here are five empty muddy lakes and you get to put objects in them. Draw three things in each lake. BUT the lake with the **A** in the middle must have objects with **a** sounds, the **E** lake must have objects with **e** sounds, and so on. Got it? (The **A** lake has been started for you.)

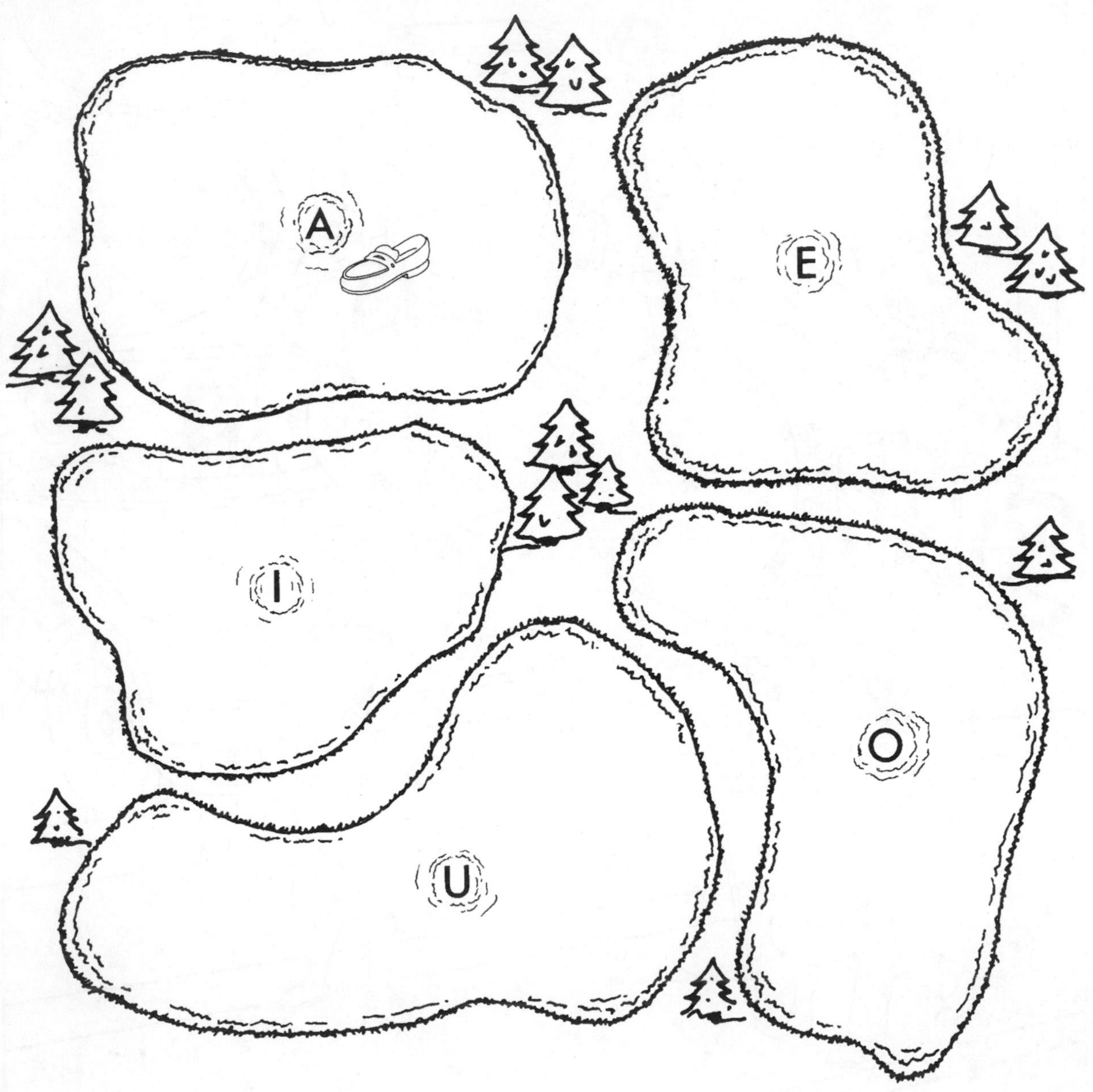

Nombre ____________________

Lección 23

¡Aquí viene el autobús!

Yo aprendo el vocabulario

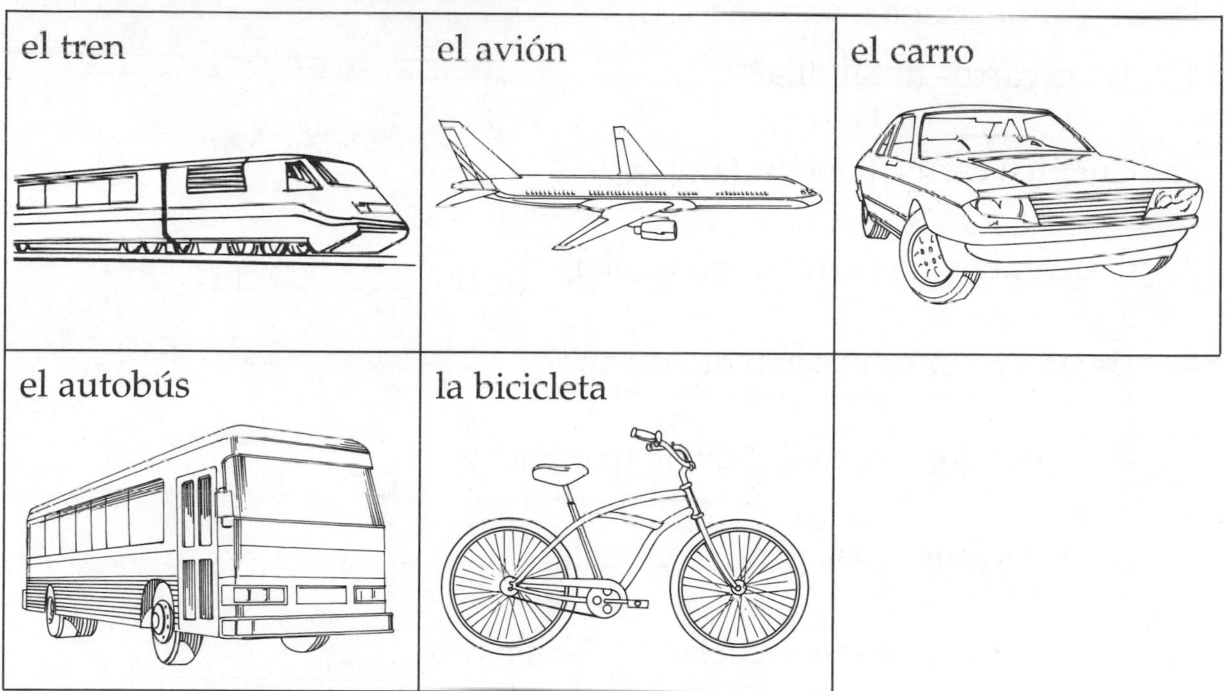

Más vocabulario

Aquí viene el autobus.

Nombre ______________________

Yo hablo

Have you ever dreamed of being a pilot and flying an airplane? Or of being a bus driver and taking people all around the city? That would be so much fun! Let's talk about different kinds of transportation. Listen to the questions and take turns answering them.

1. ¿Tiene carros tu familia?
2. ¿Cuántos carros tiene tu familia?
3. ¿Quién tiene un carro en tu familia?
4. ¿De qué color es el carro de tu papá?
5. ¿De qué color es el autobús de tu escuela?
6. ¿Cuántos autobuses tiene tu escuela?
7. ¿Hay un avión en tu escuela?
8. ¿Hay un tren en tu escuela?
9. ¿Tienes una bicicleta?
10. ¿De qué color es tu bicicleta?

Nombre ______________________________

Yo practico

Only forty-eight people live in the little town of Soledad, and they sure get excited when friends visit. They have marked on the calendar the days in March when people will arrive by car, bus, airplane, or bicycle. Look at the calendar below and take turns saying when each method of transportation comes.

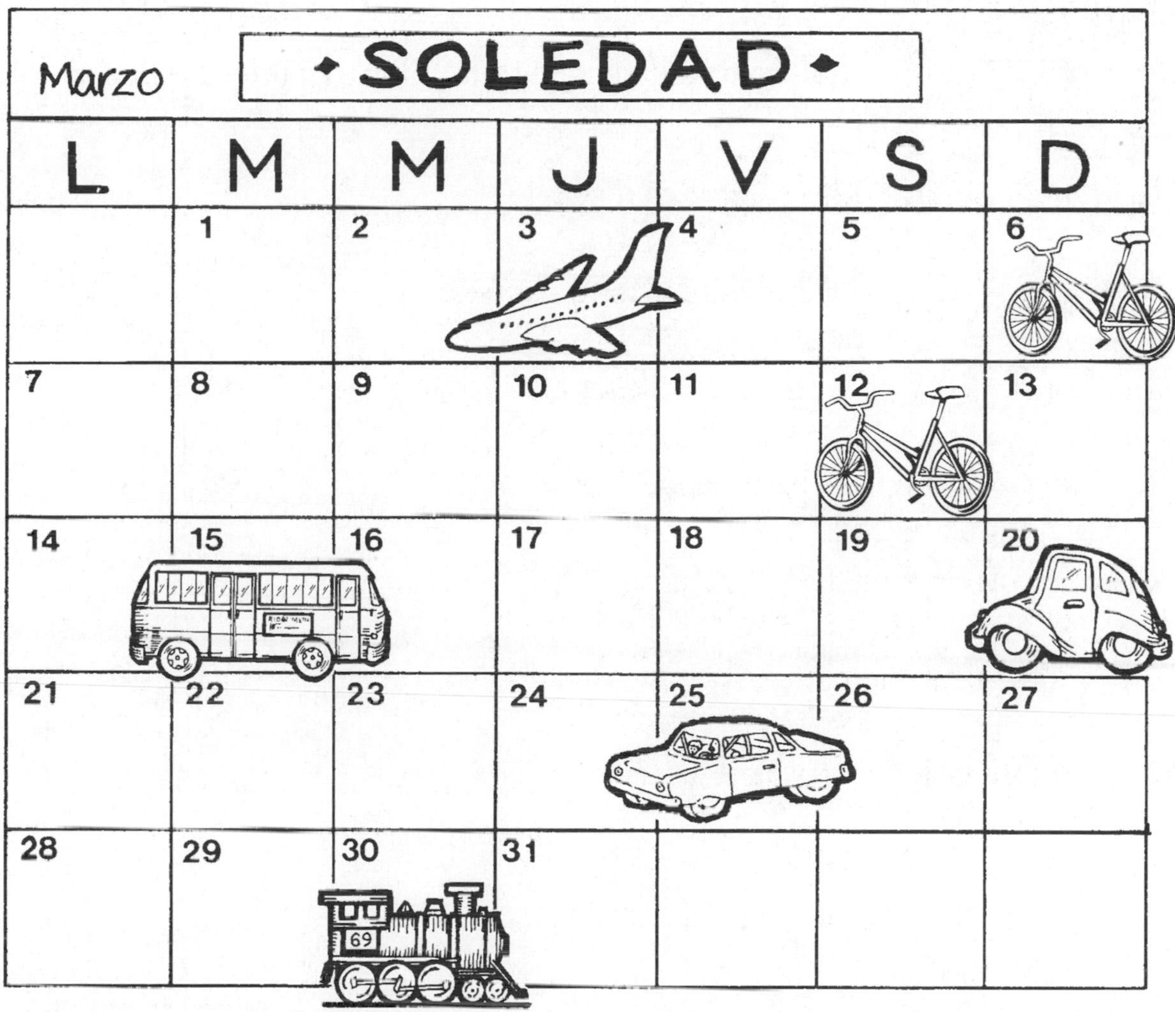

Nombre ______________________________

Yo juego

The bus, the train, the car, the plane, and the bicycle are taking things to a giant flea market.

The bus carries items with an "a" sound.
The car carries items with an "o" sound.
The train carries items with an "u" sound.
The plane carries items with an "i" sound.
The bicycle carries items with an "e" sound.

Draw a line from each item to the vehicle that will carry it to the flea market.

Nombre ______________________________

Yo imagino

Here is a long, empty road and a big, empty sky. The person at the end of the road is you, so draw in your clothes and hair. Now fill the road and sky with things that you can describe in Spanish. You may make a serious picture, like **Hay muchos niños y niñas en el autobús amarillo.** Or you may draw a silly picture, like **Hay un caballo azul en el avión.**

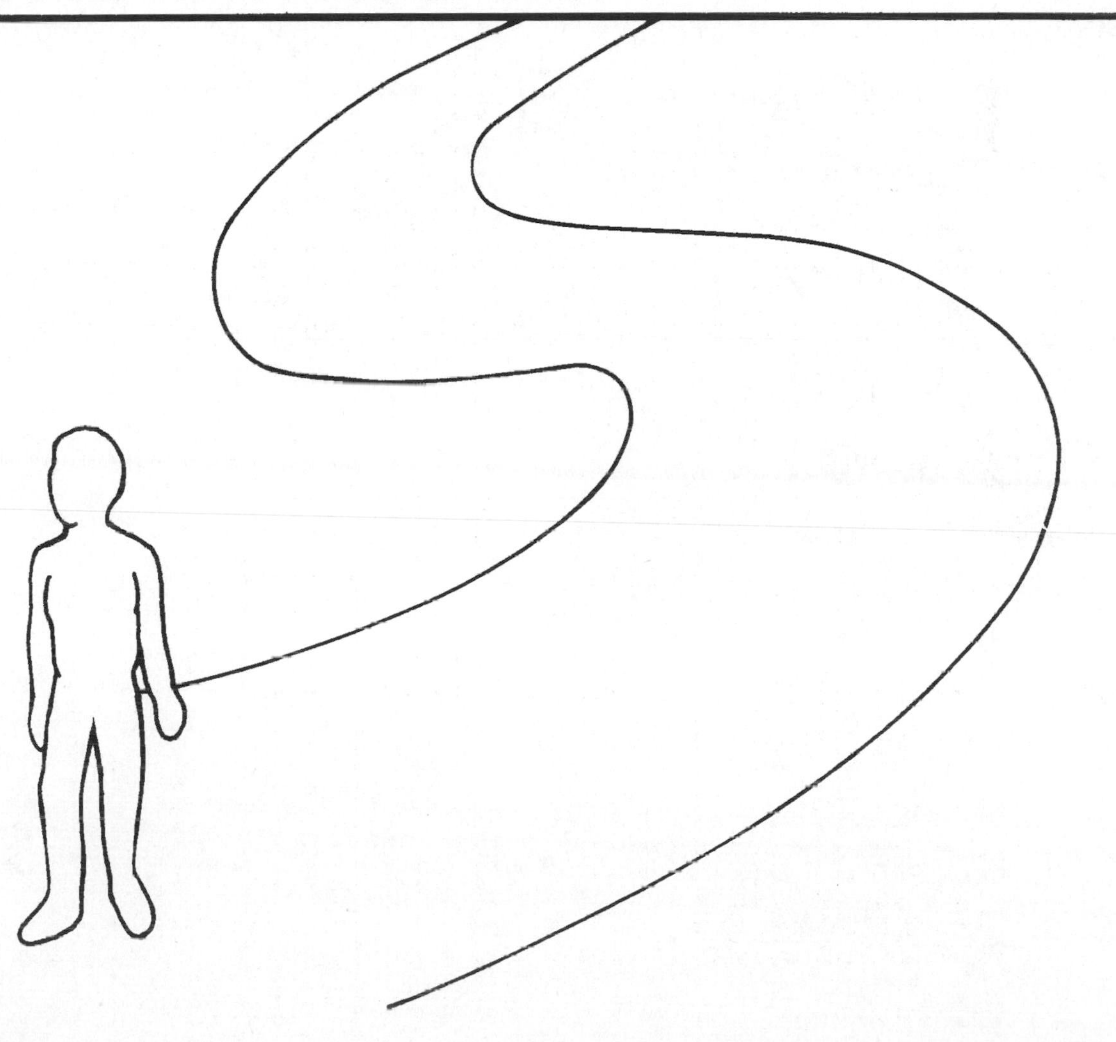

Nombre ____________________

Lección 24

¿Adónde vas?

Yo aprendo el vocabulario

Más vocabulario

¿Adónde vas?

Voy a la (al) ____.

Voy a la (al) ____ en ____.

Nombre ______________________

Yo hablo

Have you ever taken a plane to go to the movies? Of course not! That was a silly question. Everybody knows you don't take a plane to go to the movies. BUT where would you go on a plane? Where would you go in a car? Listen to the questions and take turns answering them.

1. ¿Adónde vas en bicicleta?
2. ¿Adónde vas en autobús?
3. ¿Adónde vas en carro?
4. ¿Adónde vas en tren?
5. ¿Adónde vas en avión?
6. ¿Vas en avión a la playa en México?
7. ¿Vas a la playa hoy?
8. ¿Vas al parque hoy?
9. ¿Vas a pie al parque?

Nombre ______________________

Yo practico

You are visiting your friends in Puerto Rico, and they planned fun activities for every day. Where will you go and what will you wear each day? How will you get there?

Nombre ______________________

Yo juego

On the left side of this page are some places. On the right side are ways to get to the places. Decide how you want to get to each place. Draw a line from each place to the way you will get there. You may take the same transportation to more than one place. Then take turns sharing your plans with the class.

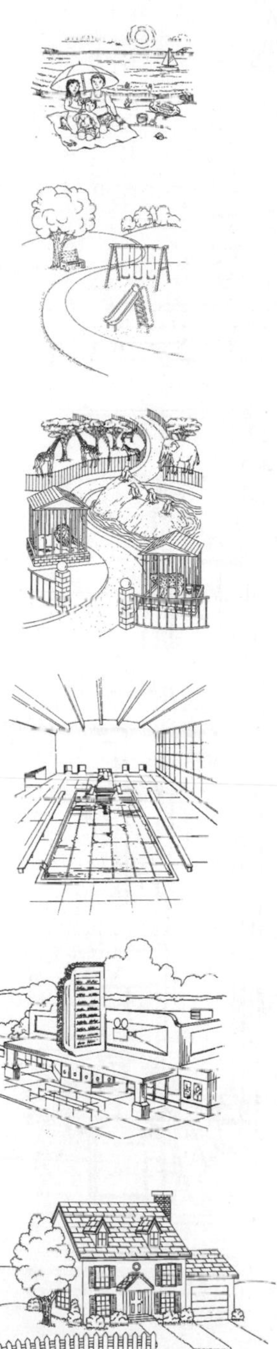

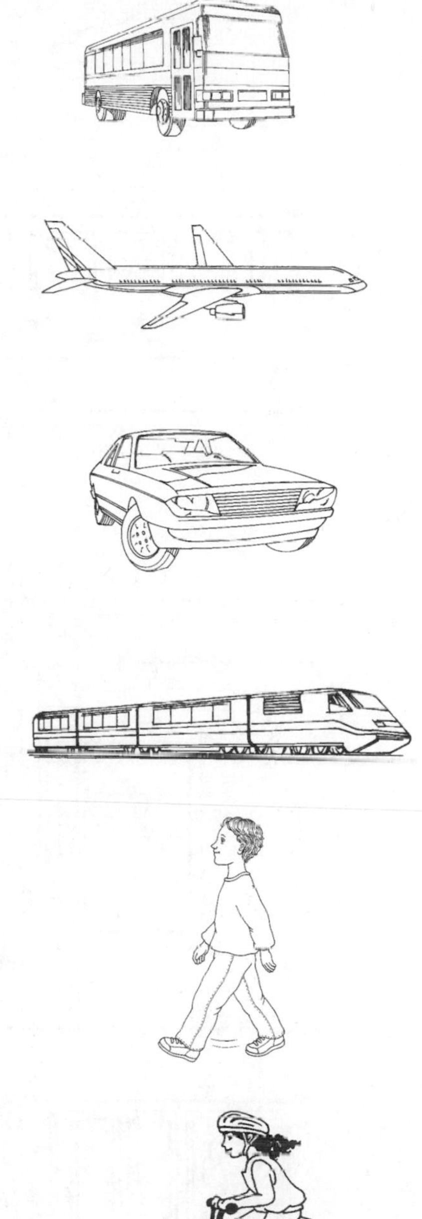

Nombre ______________________________

Yo imagino

This is your hometown, Ciudad Bonita, and you know everyone in it. Talk about the people you see here, their names, how they feel, where they are going and how they are getting there. Take turns telling your story to the class.

Nombre ______________________________

Lección 25

¡Vamos a jugar! ¡Ya llegó el verano!

Yo aprendo el vocabulario

Más vocabulario

¿Qué vas a hacer?

Voy a jugar al _____.

Voy a _____.

Nombre ______________________________

Yo hablo

The director of the new summer camp wants to know what you like to do for fun. What are your favorite activities? Where do you go to do your favorite activities? Listen to the questions and take turns answering them.

1. ¿Te gusta el fútbol?
2. ¿Te gusta el fútbol americano?
3. ¿Te gusta el béisbol?
4. ¿Te gusta saltar la cuerda?
5. ¿Vas al parque hoy?
6. ¿Qué vas a hacer en el parque?
7. ¿Vas a la piscina hoy?
8. ¿Cuándo vas a la piscina?
9. ¿Qué vas a hacer en la piscina?

Nombre ______________________

Yo practico

Señora Bustamante asked some of the children in her class what they will do this summer. Look at the pictures. Then take turns telling the class what you think each child is saying.

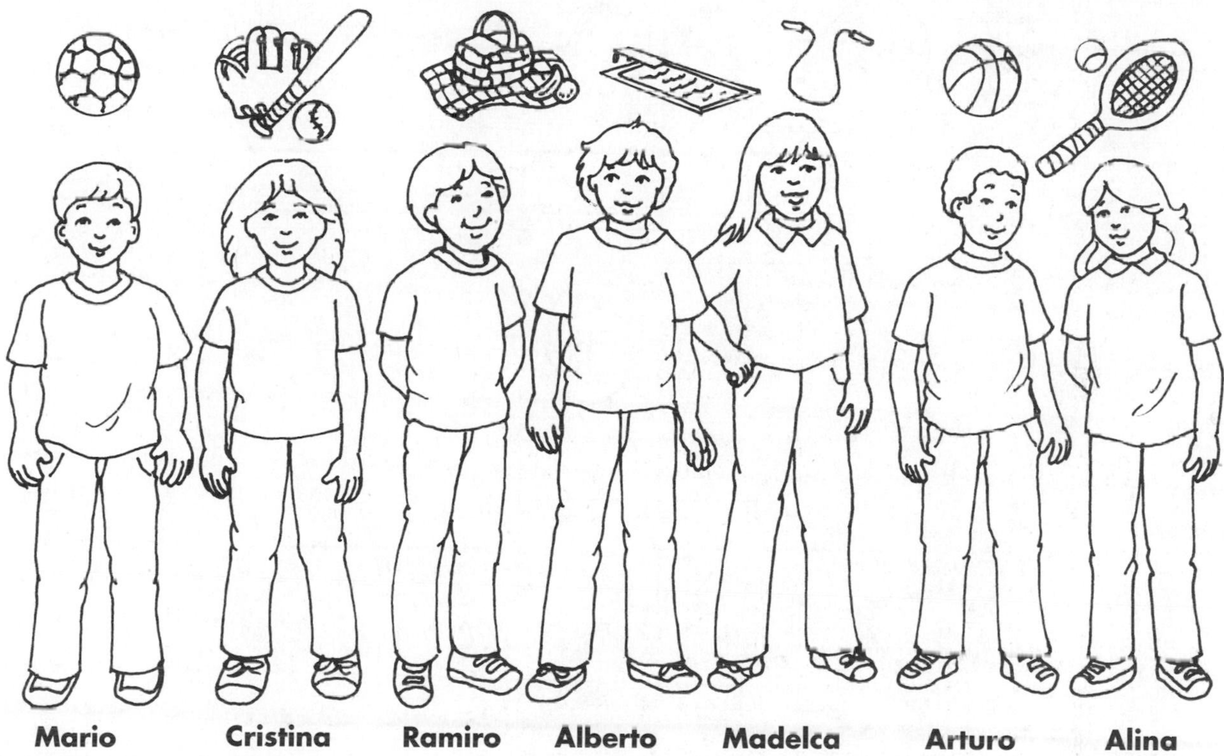

Nombre ______________________

Yo juego

Amparo has made up a puzzle about something she plans to do this summer. Look at the pictures. On the line below each word, write the first letter of the word for the picture and you will find out what Amparo is going to do.

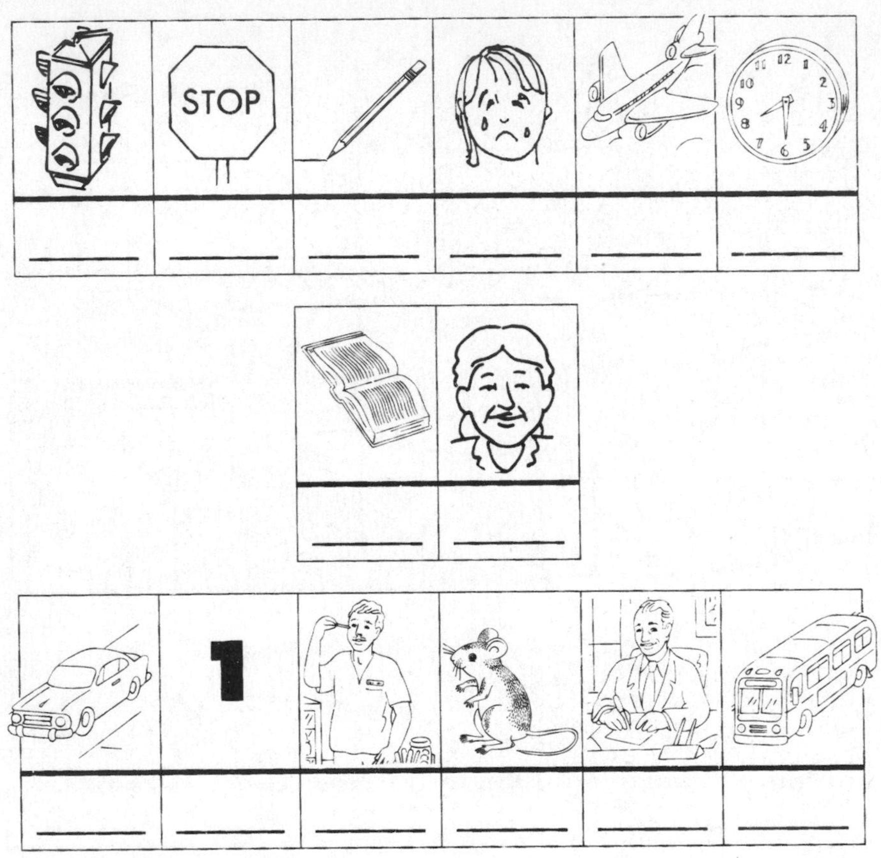

What do you talk on every day? Look at the pictures. Write the first letter of the word for each picture on the line below it to find out the answer.

Nombre ______________________________

Yo imagino

What will you and your friends do in the park this summer? Draw yourself and your friends in this park and color your picture. Then share your picture with your classmates by describing it to the class. Tell the class what you will do and what you will not do in the park.

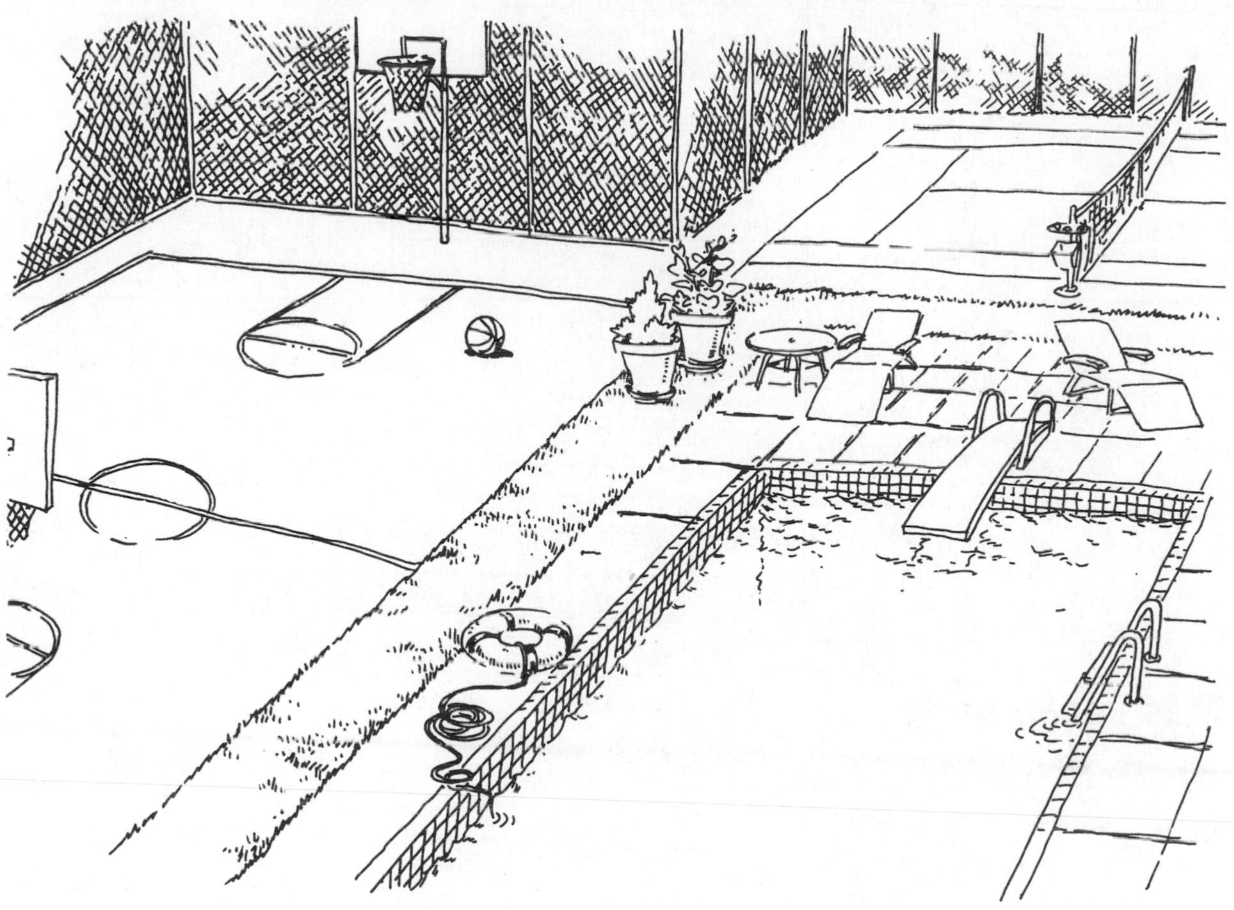

Nombre ______________________________

Lección 26

¿Qué vamos a hacer?

Yo aprendo el vocabulario

Más vocabulario

¿Qué va a hacer?

Va a ______.

Nombre ______________________

Yo hablo

What are you going to do this summer? Listen to the questions and take turns answering them.

1. ¿Tienes una bicicleta?
2. ¿Vas a andar en bicicleta en julio?
3. ¿Vas a nadar en agosto?
4. ¿Adónde vas cuando quieres nadar?
5. ¿Qué va a hacer tu familia en agosto?
6. ¿Adónde va tu familia?
7. ¿En qué va tu familia en verano?
8. ¿Qué va a hacer tu familia en verano?

Nombre ______________________________

Yo practico

Look at the picture below. Take turns saying what plans the Álvarez family and their friends Inés, María, and Pablo have for the month of June.

Nombre ______________________________

Yo juego

For this game you need a coin and a game marker. First, flip a coin. *Heads* means you move ahead one space; *tails* means you get to move ahead two spaces. Look at the space you have landed on and say **"Hace buen tiempo."** if the activity is something you could do in good weather. Say **"Hace mal tiempo."** if you would probably do the activity in bad weather. If you say the correct sentence in Spanish, you may flip the coin again. If not, you must move your game marker back a space and let the next player take a turn.

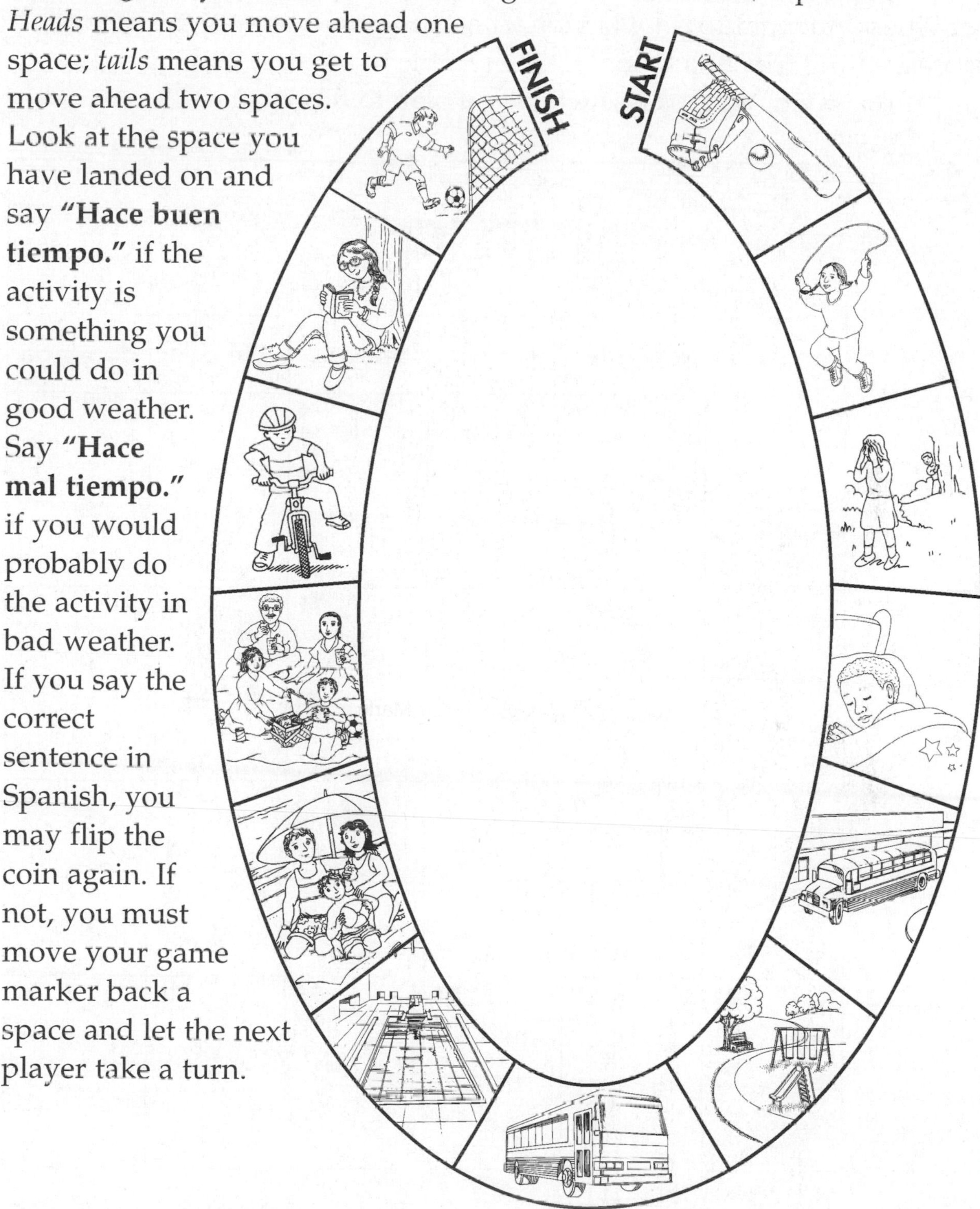

Nombre ____________________

Yo imagino

Here is a calendar for the month of June. Fill it up with pictures of activities you want to do. Plan lots of activities and be sure to schedule some exciting trips! First, look at the sample in the first two days. Then take turns saying to the class when you plan to do what.

junio						
lunes	**martes**	**miércoles**	**jueves**	**viernes**	**sábado**	**domingo**
	1	2	3	4	5	6
7	8	9	10	11	12	13
14	15	16	17	18	19	20
21 / 28	22 / 29	23 / 30	24	25	26	27

Nombre ______________________________

Lección 27

Vamos a practicar todo lo que hemos aprendido

Yo practico

A. These children need some clothes! Listen to the instructions and draw Ana and Miguel's clothing.

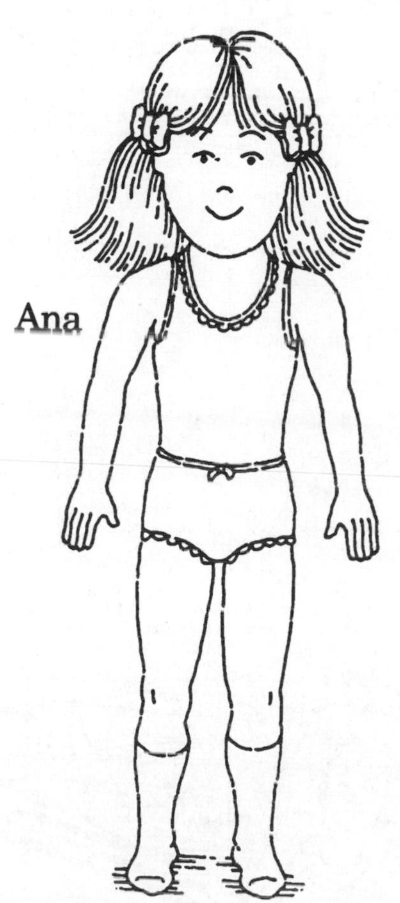

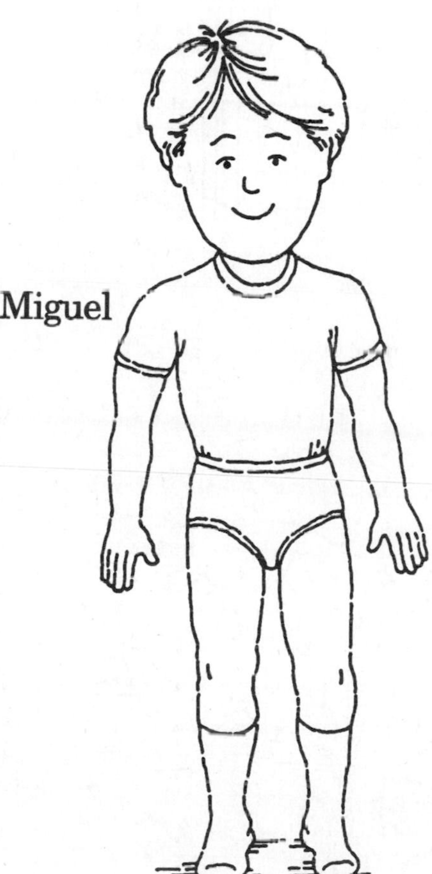

Nombre ____________________

B. Wow! What a fantastic vacation! You want to share your photos with your teacher and your classmates. Describe your photos to the class.

Nombre ______________________________

Nombre ________________________________

Yo juego

Here's a chance for you to draw a comic strip! You call your friend Leticia on her cell phone. She's at the beach, and she tells you a lot of things about what she's doing. Here's what she tells you:

- what she's wearing
- what the weather is like
- how she usually gets to the beach
- what she is going to do after the beach
- what her nose, face, and arms look like because of the sun
- how she is feeling

Make a comic strip with six panels. Draw each thing that Leticia tells you about. Then share your comic strip with your classmates, using Spanish to tell them the story about Leticia's day at the beach.

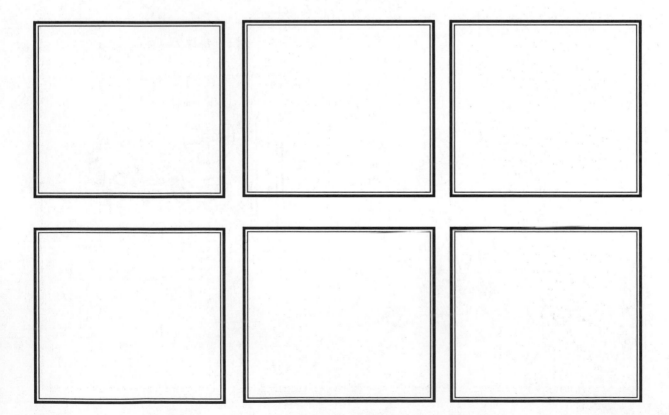

Nombre ______________________

Yo imagino

Imagine a city—the streets, the people, the buildings, the traffic lights, the police, the cars, the buses, the bicycles, the trains, and the planes in the sky. What is the weather like? What are people wearing? What colors are they are wearing? Where are they going? What are they going to do? How does each person feel? What day of the week is today? In the space below draw a city scene. Then take turns describing it to the class.

Nombre ______________________

End-of-Year Review

Vamos a practicar todo lo que hemos aprendido

Yo hablo

It's the end of the school year! You have learned a lot in Spanish class. You can say hello in Spanish, what your name is, how you are, how old you are, when your birthday is, what day it is... you can even count to 50! Wow! That's a lot, isn't it? Your teacher wants to know what you remember. Listen to his or her questions and take turns answering them.

1. ¿Cómo te llamas?
2. ¿Cómo estás?
3. ¿Cómo se llama tu mamá?
4. ¿Cómo se llama tu papá?
5. ¿Cuántos años tienes?
6. ¿Cuándo es tu cumpleaños?
7. ¿Qué día es hoy?
8. ¿Qué fecha es hoy?
9. ¿Qué tiempo hace hoy?
10. ¿Qué llevas hoy?

Nombre ______________________

Yo practico

A. What would you say in the following situations? Take turns saying it to the class.

1. It's 7:45 in the morning. You are on your way to school. You run into your neighbor, señora Fraga, who is on her way to her work. You say:

2. While you are playing in your yard, a woman stops and asks you where the bus station is. You give her directions and she thanks you. You say:

3. It's hot. You are playing soccer with your friends. You have been playing for half an hour. You feel like drinking lots of water. You say:

4. It's 3:25 in the afternoon. You are almost home from school and you want to get there before a cartoon that you like comes on at 3:30. You run into a couple of friends who stop to say hello, but you have to keep walking. You say:

5. It's not hot. It's not cold. It's not windy. It's sunny and pleasant. You say:

6. You just learned that the art project you worked on was chosen among the three best in your class. You say to your partners:

7. Your cousins from Texas were visiting your family for a week. They are sitting with their parents in a taxi in front of your house. They are about to leave for the airport to fly back to Texas. The taxi starts moving and your cousins wave farewell. You say to them:

8. You are in math class. You forgot your ruler at home. You need one, though, to do an activity in your math workbook. The teacher gives you a ruler. You say to her:

Nombre ___________________________

B. Listen to the instructions. Then look at each set of pictures and follow the instructions.

Nombre ______________________

Yo juego

A. Let's play a game. The pictures below show the different rooms of your school. Draw two things that belong in each room, and two things that don't belong there. Then take turns describing to the class where you put each item. There's a horse in the classroom? There's a pair of shoes on your teacher's desk? You choose! Who can come up with the silliest things of all?

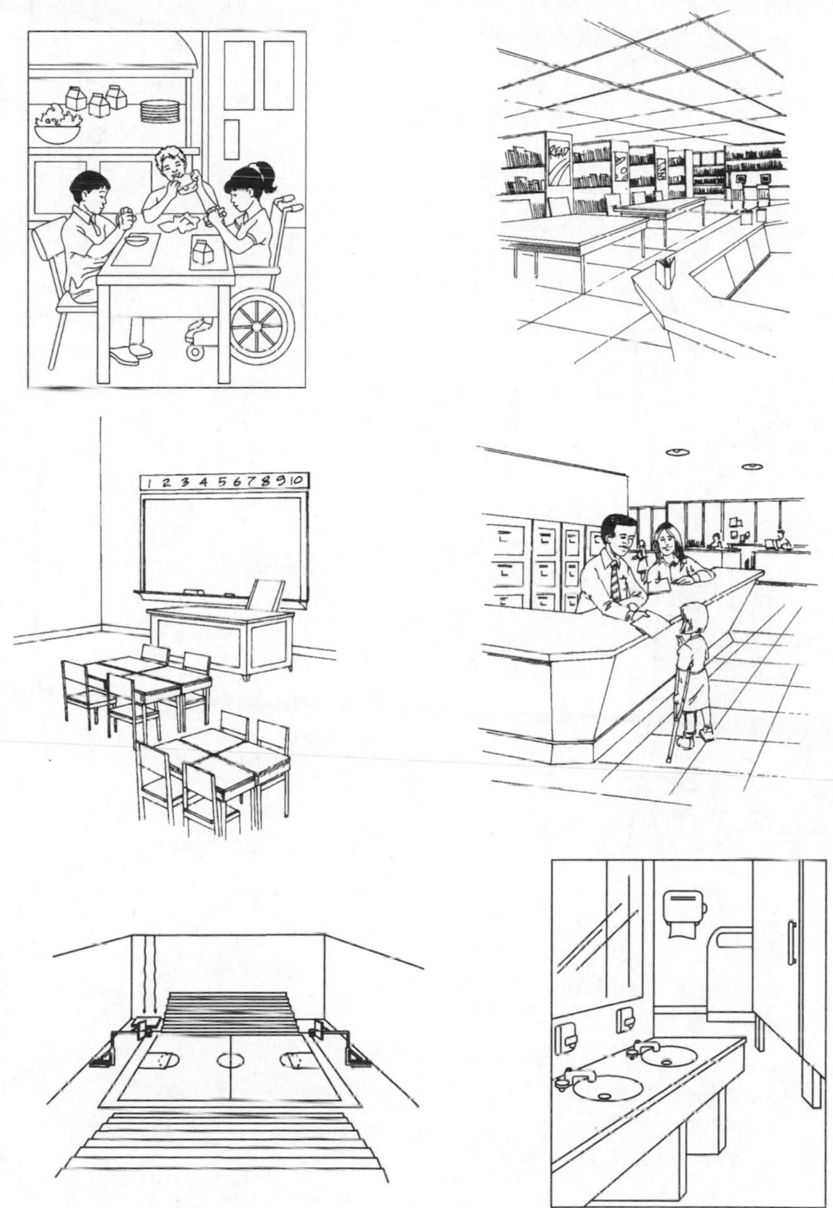

Nombre ______________________________

B. Play this game with a partner or a small group. You need a coin and a game marker. First, flip a coin. *Heads* means you move ahead one space; *tails* means you get to move ahead two spaces. Look at the space you have landed on and say in Spanish what is shown. It could be a place, an activity, or something you ride in or on. If you say the correct words in Spanish, you may flip the coin again. If not, you must move your game marker back a space and let the next player take a turn.

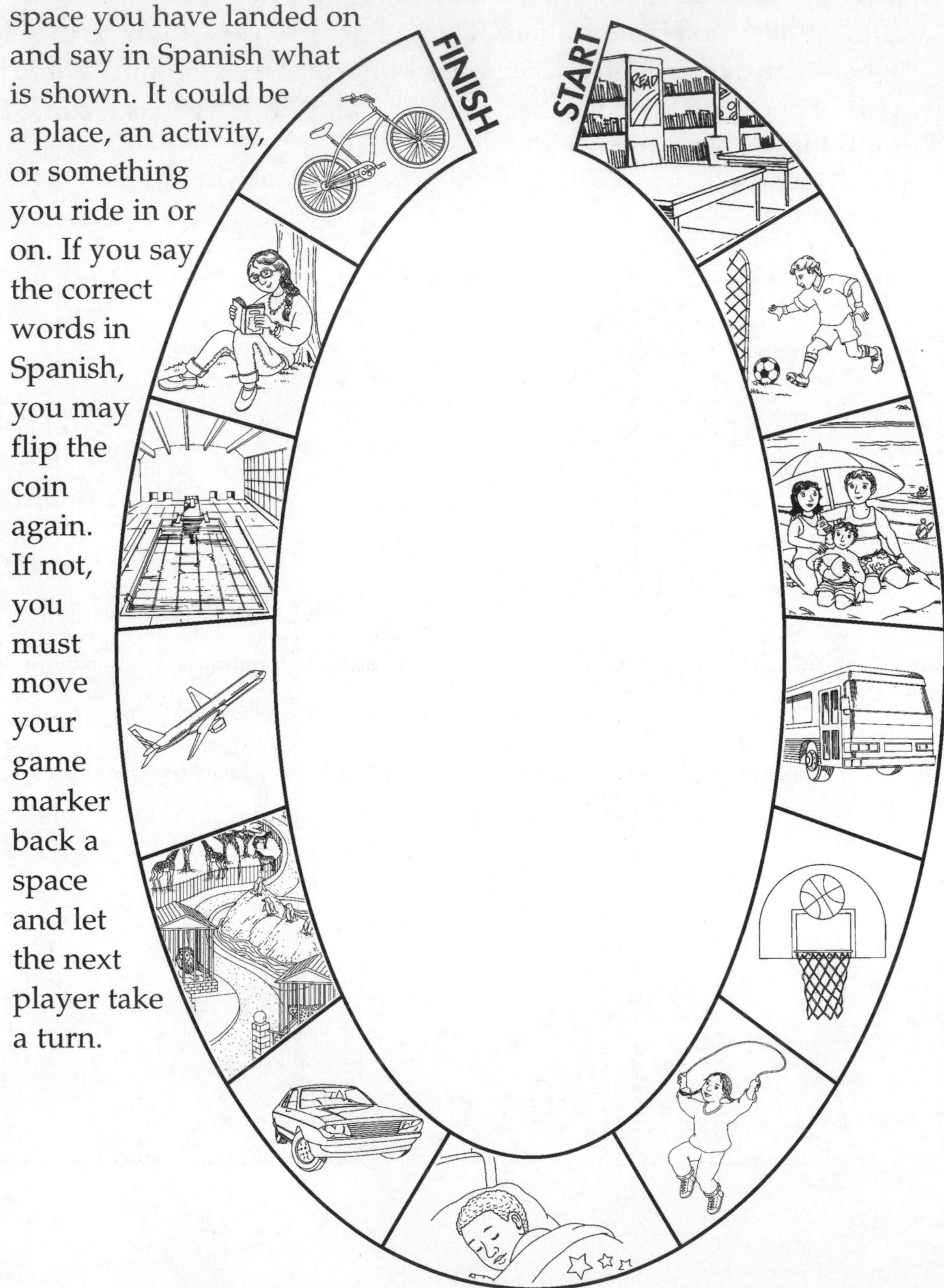

Nombre ______________________________

Yo imagino

Imagine your dream vacation. Think of places you would like to go and of activities you would like to do. Think also of the people with whom you would like to go and how you would get there. Think of the weather and of how people feel in different weather. Remember, this is your dream vacation. So, feel free to plan going to as many places as you wish and doing as many things as you like. In the boxes below, draw six scenes of your dream vacation. Then take turns describing your dream vacation to the class.

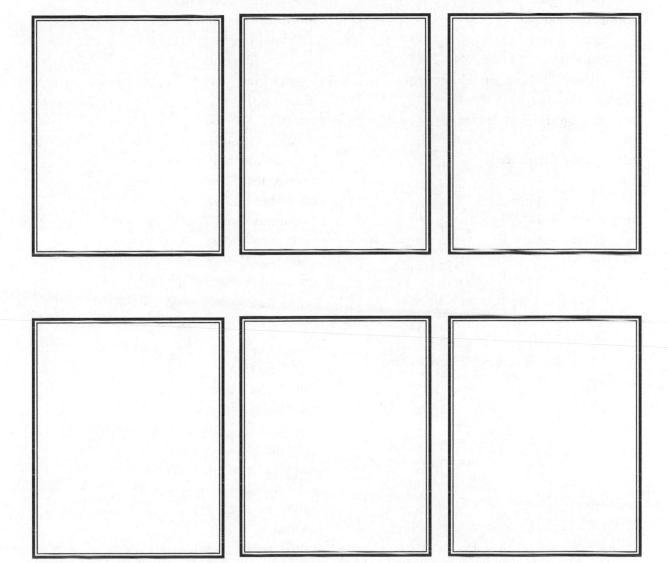

Spanish–English Glossary

A

a to, at
a pie walking, by foot
abril April
abuela, la grandmother
abuelo, el grandfather
Adiós. Goodbye.
¿adónde? (to) where?
¿Adónde vas? ¿Adónde va usted? Where are you going?
agosto August
agrupa group *(command)*
ahora now
¡alto! stop *(command)*
alto (-a) tall
amarillo (-a) yellow
amiga, la friend *(f.)*
amigo, el friend *(m.)*
amigos, los friends
anaranjado (-a) orange (color)
andar en bicicleta to ride a bicycle
animal, el animal
año, el year
¿Cuántos años tienes? How old are you?
Tengo ____ años. I am ____ years old.
aquí here
¡Aquí está! Here it is!
Aquí viene ____. Here comes ____.
así, así so-so
autobús, el bus
avión, el plane
azul blue

B

bajo (-a) short
baloncesto, el basketball
bandera, la flag
bate beat (cooking) *(command)*
béisbol, el baseball
biblioteca, la library
bicicleta, la bicycle
bien well, good
muy bien very well, very good
blanco (-a) white
blusa, la blouse
boca, la mouth
bonito (-a) pretty
brazos, los arms
buen, bueno (-a) good
Buenos días. Good morning.
Buenas noches. Good night.
Buenas tardes. Good afternoon.
busca look for, search *(command)*

C

caballo, el horse
cabeza, la head
cafetería, la lunchroom, cafeteria
calcetines, los socks
calendario, el calendar
caliente hot
calle, la street
camisa, la shirt
camiseta, la T-shirt
cantar to sing
Vamos a cantar. Let's sing.

cara, la face
carro, el car
catorce fourteen
cerdo, el pig
cero zero
chaqueta, la jacket
chocolate, el chocolate
cinco five
cincuenta fifty
cine, el movie theater
círculo, el circle
clase, la class
color, el color
¿De qué color es? What color is it?
colorear to color
colorea color *(command)*
¿cómo? how? what?
¿Cómo estás? How are you?
¿Cómo se llama ____? What's the ____ called?; What's ____ name?
¿Cómo se llama usted? What's your name? *(formal)*
¿Cómo te llamas? What's your name? *(familiar)*
computadora, la computer
con with
conejo, el rabbit
contar to count
cuenta count *(command)*
Vamos a contar. Let's count.
contento (-a) happy
Estoy contento (-a). I'm happy.
creyón, el crayon
cruzar to cross
Cruzo la calle. I cross the street.
cuadrado, el square
¿cuál? what? which?
¿Cuál falta? Which (one) is missing? What's missing?
¿cuándo? when?
¿Cuándo es tu cumpleaños? When is your birthday?
¿cuántos (-as)? how many?
¿Cuántos / Cuántas (días, semanas, meses) hay? How many (days, weeks, months) are there?
¿Cuántos años tiene? How old is he/she?
¿Cuántos años tienes? How old are you?
¿Cuántos tengo? How many do I have?
cuarenta forty
cuarenta y uno . . . cuarenta y nueve forty-one . . . forty-nine
cuarto de baño, el bathroom
cuatro four
cumpleaños, el birthday
¿Cuándo es tu cumpleaños? When is your birthday?
Mi cumpleaños es el ____ de ____. My birthday is the ____ of ____.

D

dale give him/her *(command)*
dame give me *(command)*
de of, from
De nada. You're welcome
decir to say
Dice «____». He/She/It says "____".
dice he/she/it says
dicen they say
¿Qué dice ____? What does ____ say?
dedos, los fingers
derecha, la right (direction)
Miro a la derecha. I look to the right.
despacio slowly
día, el day
Buenos días. Good morning.
¿Qué día es hoy? What day is today?
dibuja draw *(command)*
dibuja una línea draw a line *(command)*
diciembre December
diecinueve nineteen
dieciocho eighteen
dieciséis sixteen
diecisiete seventeen
diez ten
director, el principal *(m.)*
directora, la principal *(f.)*
doce twelve
dolor, el pain
Tengo dolor. I hurt. I'm in pain.

domingo, el Sunday
¿dónde? where?
  ¿Dónde está ____? Where is ____?
  ¿Dónde están ____? Where are ____?
dormir to sleep
dos two

E

el the
él he
ella she
en in, on, into, at
enero January
enfermera, la nurse *(f.)*
enfermero, el nurse *(m.)*
enojado (-a) angry
  Estoy enojado (-a). I'm angry.
Es el ____. It's the ____.
Es un (una) ____. It's a ____.
Es ____. It's ____.
escritorio, el desk
escuela, la school
espera wait *(command)*
esta, este this
ésta, éste this one
estar to be
  está he, she, it is
    Está en ____. He/She/It is in ____.
    Está lloviendo. It's raining.
    Está nevando. It's snowing.
  están you are, they are
    Están en ____. They are in ____.
  estás you are
  estoy I'm
    Estoy (muy) bien. I'm (very) well.
    Estoy (muy) mal. I feel (very) bad.
    Estoy así, así. I'm so-so.
    Estoy contento (-a). I'm happy.
    Estoy enojado (-a). I'm angry.
    Estoy más o menos. I'm okay, more or less.
    Estoy pensando en . . . I'm thinking of . . .
    Estoy triste. I'm sad.
esto this

F

falda, la skirt
familia, la family
febrero February
fecha, la date (calendar)
  ¿Qué fecha es hoy? What's the date?
feo (-a) ugly
fiesta, la party
figura, la shape
frío (-a) cold (adjective)
frío, el cold (noun)
  Hace frío. It's cold.
  Tengo frío. I'm cold.
fútbol, el soccer
fútbol americano, el football

G

gafas de sol, las sunglasses
gallina, la hen
gallo, el rooster
gato, el cat
gimnasio, el gym
globo, el globe
Gracias. Thank you.
grande large, big
granja, la farm
gris gray

hablar to speak
  Hablo por teléfono. I'm talking on the telephone.

hacer to make, to do

Hace ____. It's ____.

Hace buen tiempo. The weather is good.

Hace calor. It's hot.

Hace frío. It's cold.

Hace mal tiempo. The weather is bad.

Hace sol. It's sunny.

Hace viento. It's windy.

¿Qué haces? What are you doing?

¿Qué va a hacer? What is he/she going to do?

¿Qué vas a hacer? ¿Qué va a hacer usted? What are you going to do?

hacer un viaje to take a trip

hasta until, to

Hasta la vista. See you later!

¡Hasta luego! See you later!

¡Hasta mañana! See you tomorrow!

¡Hasta pronto! See you soon!

hay there is, there are

hermana, la sister

hermanastra, la stepsister

hermanastro, el stepbrother

hermano, el brother

hija, la daughter

hijo, el son

¡Hola! Hello!

hoy today

Hoy es ____. Today is ____.

Hoy es el ____. Today is the ____.

¿Qué día es hoy? What day is today?

I

ir to go

¿Qué va a hacer? What is he/she/it going to do?

¿Qué vas a hacer? What are you going to do?

Va a ____. He/She/It is going to ____.

Vamos a ____. Let's ____.

ve go *(command)*

Voy a ____. I'm going to ____.

Voy a ____ en ____. I'm going to ____ by ____.

Voy a jugar al ____. I'm going to play ____.

ir de picnic to go on a picnic

izquierda, la left (direction)

Miro a la izquierda. I look to the left.

J

jueves, el Thursday

jugar to play (a game)

Voy a jugar al ____. I'm going to play ____.

julio July

junio June

L

la the *(f.)*

lápiz, el pencil

las the *(f. pl.)*

lástima pity

¡Qué lástima! What a pity!

leer to read

libro, el book

llamarse to be called, named

me llamo my name is

se llama his/her/its name is

te llamas your name is

llevar to wear

lleva he/she is wearing; you're wearing

llevas you're wearing

llevo I'm wearing

Llevo (un, una, unos, unas) ____. I'm wearing a ____.

¿Qué llevas? What are you wearing? What do you have on?

llover to rain

Está lloviendo. It's raining.

lobo, el wolf
los the *(m. pl.)*
luego later
lunes, el Monday
luz, la light

M

madrastra, la stepmother
madre, la mother
maestra, la teacher *(f.)*
maestro, el teacher *(m.)*
mal; malo (-a) bad; not well
  Estoy (muy) mal. I feel (very) bad.
mamá, la mom
manos, las hands
mañana, la morning; tomorrow
  Hasta mañana. See you tomorrow.
  Mañana es ____. Tomorrow is ____.
mapa, el map
Marca el número ____. Dial the number ____.
marcador, el marker
marrón brown
martes, el Tuesday
marzo March
mayo May
mediano (-a) medium
Me llamo ____. My name is ____.
mes, el; meses, los month, months
mesa, la table
mi, mis my
miércoles, el Wednesday
mirar to look
  mira look *(command)*
  Miro a la derecha. I look to the right.
  Miro a la izquierda. I look to the left.
morado (-a) purple
mostrar to bring
  muéstrame show me *(command)*
mucho (-a) much, very
muy very

N

nadar to swim
nariz, la nose
negro (-a) black
nevar to snow
  Está nevando. It's snowing.
niña, la girl
niños, los children
niño, el boy
no no
noche, la night
  Buenas noches. Good night.
noviembre November
nueve nine
nuevo (-a) new
número, el number
  ¿Qué número es? What number is it?

o or
ocho eight
octágono, el octagon
octubre October
oficina, la office
ojos, los eyes
once eleven
orejas, las ears
oveja, la sheep *(s.)*

P

padrastro, el stepfather
padre, el father
pájaro, el bird
pantalones, los pants
  pantalones cortos, los shorts
papá, el dad
papel, el paper
para for, to

parque, el park
patio de recreo, el playground
pato, el duck
pelo, el hair
pensar to think
Estoy pensando en . . . I'm thinking of . . .
pequeño (-a) small
perro, el dog
persona, la person
personas, las people
piernas, las legs
pies, los feet
pijama, el pajamas
piscina, la swimming pool
pizarrón, el chalkboard
playa, la beach
policía, el police officer *(m.)*
policía, la police officer *(f.)*
poner to put
pon put *(command)*
Pon un círculo. Draw a circle.
Pon una X. Draw an X.
por for, by, through
Por favor. Please.
practicar to practice
primero first
¿Puedo ir? May I go?
pupitre, el student desk

Q

que who; which, that
¿Qué? What?
¿De qué color es? What color is it?
¿Qué día es hoy? What day is today?
¿Qué dice ____? What does ____ say?
¿Qué es? What is this?
¿Qué fecha es hoy? What's the date?
¿Qué figura es? What shape is it?
¿Qué haces? What are you doing?
¿Qué llevas? What are you wearing? What do you have on?
¿Qué número es? What number is it?
¿Qué son? What are these?
¿Qué tal? What's up? How's it going?
¿Qué tiempo hace (hoy)? What's the weather like (today)?
¿Qué tiene ____? What does ____ have?
¿Qué va a hacer? What is he/she going to do?
¿Qué vas a hacer? ¿Qué va a hacer? What are you going to do?
¡qué! how! what!
¡Qué bonito (-a)! How pretty!
¡Qué bueno! How wonderful!
¡Qué lástima! What a pity! What a shame!
¿quién? who?
¿Quién es? Who is it?
¿Quién tiene ____? Who has ____.
quince fifteen
quita take away *(command)*

R

rana, la frog
rápido quickly
ratón, el mouse
rectángulo, el rectangle
regla, la ruler
reloj, el clock
rojo (-a) red
rosado (-a) pink

S

sábado, el Saturday
salón de clases, el classroom
saltar to jump
salta jump *(command)*
saltar la cuerda jump rope

Se llama ____. His/Her/It's name is ____.
secretaria, la secretary *(f.)*
secretario, el secretary *(m.)*
seis six
sentir to feel
Lo siento mucho. I'm very sorry.
semáforo, el traffic light
semana, la week
sentarse to sit down
siéntate sit down *(command)*
señor Mr.
señora Mrs.
señorita Miss
septiembre September
ser to be
es he/she/it is; you are *(formal)*
son they are
sí yes
siete seven
sigue go *(command)*
silla, la chair
sombrero, el hat
Son ____. They are ____.
su, sus his/her/its/your, their
suéter, el sweater

T

también also, too
tarde, la afternoon
Buenas tardes. Good afternoon.
teléfono, el telephone
teléfono celular, el cellular telephone
tener to have
tengo I have
Tengo ____ años. I'm ____ years old.
Tengo calor. I'm hot.
Tengo dolor. I hurt.; I'm in pain.; I have a pain.
Tengo frío. I'm cold.
Tengo hambre. I'm hungry.
Tengo miedo. I'm afraid.; I'm scared.
Tengo prisa. I'm in a hurry.
Tengo sed. I'm thirsty.
Tengo sueño. I'm sleepy.
Tengo suerte. I'm lucky.
tiene he/she/it has
Tiene ____ años. He/She/It is ____ years old.
¿Tienes ____? Do you have ____?
tenis, el tennis
ti you
tiempo, el weather
Hace buen tiempo. The weather is good.
Hace mal tiempo. The weather is bad.
¿Qué tiempo hace hoy? What's the weather today?
títere, el puppet
tiza, la chalk
tocar to touch
toca touch *(command)*
toma take *(command)*
tráeme bring me *(command)*
traje de baño, el bathing suit
trece thirteen
treinta thirty
treinta y uno . . . treinta y nueve thirty-one . . . thirty-nine
tren, el train
tres three
triángulo, el triangle
triste sad
Estoy triste. I'm sad.
tu your
tú you *(familiar)*

U

un, una a, an, one
un, uno, una one
usted you *(formal)*
ustedes you *(pl.)*

V

Va a ____. He/She/It is going to ____.
vaca, la cow
Vamos a ____. Let's ____.
ve go *(command)*
veinte twenty
  veintiuno . . . veintinueve twenty-one . . . twenty-nine
ventana, la window
verano, el summer
verde green
vestido, el dress
viaje, el trip
  hacer un viaje to take a trip
viento, el wind
viernes, el Friday
Voy a (al) ____ a (en) ____. I'm going ____ by ____.
Voy a (al) ____. I'm going to ____.
Voy a jugar al ____. I'm going to play ____.

Y

y and
ya already
yo I

Z

zapatos, los shoes
zoológico, el zoo

English–Spanish Glossary

A

afternoon la tarde
Good afternoon. Buenas tardes.
airplane el avión
already ya
also también
an un, una
and y
angry enojado (-a)
I'm angry. Estoy enojado (-a).
animal el animal
April abril
are está, están, es, son
How are you? ¿Cómo estás? ¿Cómo está usted?
there are hay
arms los brazos
at a, en
August agosto

B

bad, badly mal; malo
I feel bad. Estoy mal.
baseball el béisbol
basketball el baloncesto
bathing suit el traje de baño
bathroom el cuarto de baño
be, to estar, ser
he/she/it is está; es
I am estoy, soy
they are están, son
you are eres *(familiar)*; es *(formal)* estás *(familiar)*; está *(formal)*
beach la playa
beat bate (cooking) *(command)*
bicycle la bicicleta
bird el pájaro
birthday el cumpleaños
My birthday is the ____ of ____. Mi cumpleaños es el ____ de ____.
When is your birthday? ¿Cuándo es tu cumpleaños?
black negro (-a)
blouse la blusa
blue azul
book el libro
boy el niño
bring me tráeme *(command)*
brother el hermano
brown marrón
bus el autobús
by por

C

cafeteria la cafetería
calendar el calendario
called, to be llamarse
car el carro
cat el gato
cellular telephone el teléfono celular
chair la silla
chalk la tiza
chalkboard el pizarrón
chicken el pollo

child el niño, la niña
children los niños
chocolate el chocolate
circle el círculo
class la clase
classroom el salón de clases
clock el reloj
cold (adjective) frío, (-a)
cold (noun) el frío
  I'm cold. Tengo frío.
  It's cold. Hace frío.
color el color
  What color is it? ¿De qué color es?
color, to colorear
  color colorea *(command)*
computer la computadora
count, to contar
  count cuenta *(command)*
  Let's count. Vamos a contar.
cow la vaca
crayon el creyón
cross, to cruzar
  cross cruza *(command)*
  I cross the street. Cruzo la calle.

D

dad el papá
date la fecha
  What is the date? ¿Qué fecha es hoy?
daughter la hija
day el día
  the days of the week los días de la semana
  What day is today? ¿Qué día es hoy?
December diciembre
desk el escritorio
do, to hacer
  What are you doing? ¿Qué haces? ¿Qué hace usted?
  What are you going to do? ¿Qué vas a hacer? ¿Qué va a hacer usted?
  What is he (she, it) going to do? ¿Qué va a hacer?
dog el perro
draw, to dibujar
  Draw a line. Dibuja una línea. *(command)*
  Draw a circle. Pon un círculo. *(command)*
  Draw an X. Pon una X. *(command)*
dress el vestido
duck el pato

E

ears las orejas
eight ocho
eighteen dieciocho
eleven once
eyes los ojos

F

face la cara
family la familia
farm la granja
fast rápido
father el papá, el padre
February febrero
feel, to sentir
  I'm very sorry. Lo siento mucho.
  I feel (very) bad. Estoy (muy) mal.
feet los pies
fifteen quince
fifty cincuenta
finger el dedo
first primero
five cinco

flag la bandera
foot, by a pie
for para, por
forty cuarenta
forty-one . . . forty-nine cuarenta y uno . . . cuarenta y nueve
four cuatro
fourteen catorce
Friday el viernes
friend(s) la amiga *(f.)*; el amigo *(m.)*; los amigos *(pl.)*
frog la rana
from de

G

girl la niña
give, to dar
give him/her dale *(command)*
give me dame *(command)*
globe el globo
go, to ir
go sigue, ve *(command)*
I'm going to ____. Voy a ____.
I'm going to ____ by ____. Voy a ____ en ____.
What are you going to do? ¿Qué vas a hacer? ¿Qué va a hacer usted?
What is he/she going to do? ¿Qué va a hacer?
Where are you going? ¿Adónde vas? ¿Adónde va usted?
go bike riding, to andar en bicicleta
good bueno, bien
Good afternoon. Buenas tardes.
Good morning. Buenos días.
Good night. Buenas noches.
Goodbye. Adiós.
go on a picnic ir de picnic
grandfather el abuelo
grandmother la abuela
gray gris
green verde
group, to agrupar
group agrupa *(command)*
gym el gimnasio

H

hair el pelo
hands las manos
happy contento (-a)
I'm happy. Estoy contento (-a).
hat el sombrero
have, to tener
I have tengo; yo tengo
he/she/it has tiene
you have tienes *(familiar)*, tiene *(formal)*
Who has ____? ¿Quién tiene?
he él
head la cabeza
hello hola
hen la gallina
her su, sus
here aquí
Here comes ____. Aquí viene ____.
Here it is! ¡Aquí está!
hi hola
his su, sus
horse el caballo
hot caliente
how? ¿cómo?
How are you? ¿Cómo estás? ¿Cómo está usted?
How old are you? ¿Cuántos años tienes?
How old is he (she)? ¿Cuántos años tiene?
how! ¡qué!
How pretty! ¡Qué bonito (-a)!
How wonderful! ¡Qué bueno!

how many? ¿cuántos (-as)?
How many do I have? ¿Cuántos tengo?

I

I yo
I'm afraid. Tengo miedo.
I'm angry. Estoy enojado (-a).
I'm cold. Tengo frío.
I'm happy. Estoy contento (-a).
I'm hot. Tengo calor.
I'm hungry. Tengo hambre.
I'm in pain. Tengo dolor.
I hurt. Tengo dolor.
I'm in a hurry. Tengo prisa.
I'm lucky. Tengo suerte.
I'm not (very) well. No estoy (muy) bien.
I'm sad. Estoy triste.
I'm scared. Tengo miedo.
I'm sleepy. Tengo sueño.
I'm so-so. Estoy así, así.
I'm thirsty. Tengo sed.
I'm very well. Estoy (muy) bien.
I'm ____ years old. Tengo ____ años.
in en
into en
is es, está
there is hay

J

jacket la chaqueta
January enero
July julio
jump, to saltar
jump salta *(command)*
jump rope, to saltar la cuerda
June junio

L

large grande
later luego
left (direction) la izquierda
I look to the left. Miro a la izquierda.
legs las piernas
Let's ____. Vamos a ____.
Let's count. Vamos a contar.
Let's sing. Vamos a cantar.
library la biblioteca
light la luz
look, to mirar
I look to the left. Miro a la izquierda.
I look to the right. Miro a la derecha.
look mira *(command),*
look for busca *(command)*
lunchroom la cafetería

M

make, to hacer
many muchos (-as)
How many? ¿Cuántos (-as)?
map el mapa
March marzo
marker el marcador
May mayo
May I go? ¿Puedo ir?
medium mediano (-a)
Miss señorita
mom la mamá
Monday el lunes
month; months el mes; los meses
morning la mañana
Good morning. Buenos días.
mother la madre, la mamá
mouse el ratón
mouth la boca
movie theater el cine

Mr. señor
Mrs. señora
much mucho (-a)
my mi, mis

N

named, to be llamarse
  his (her) name is se llama
  my name is me llamo
  your name is te llamas
new nuevo (-a)
night la noche
  Good night. Buenas noches.
nine nueve
nineteen diecinueve
no no
nose la nariz
not no
November noviembre
now ahora
number el número
  What number is this? ¿Qué número es?
nurse el enfermero *(m.)*, la enfermera *(f.)*

O

October octubre
octagon el octágono
of de
office la oficina
on en
one un, uno, una
or o
orange (color) anaranjado (-a)

P

pain el dolor
  I'm in pain. Tengo dolor.
pajamas el pijama
pants los pantalones
paper el papel
park el parque
party la fiesta
pencil el lápiz
people las personas, la gente
person la persona
pig el cerdo
pink rosado (-a)
pity lástima
  What a pity! ¡Qué lástima!
play, to (a game) jugar
  I'm going to play ____. Voy a jugar al ____.
playground el patio de recreo
please por favor
police officer el policía, la policía
pretty bonito (-a)
principal el director, la directora
puppet el títere
purple morado (-a)
put, to poner
  put pon *(command)*

R

rabbit el conejo
rain, to llover
  It's raining. Está lloviendo.
read, to leer
rectangle el rectángulo
red rojo (-a)

ride a bike, to andar en bicicleta
right (direction) la derecha
  I look to the right. Miro a la derecha.
rooster el gallo
ruler la regla

S

sad triste
  I'm sad. Estoy triste.
Saturday el sábado
say, to decir
  he/she/it says dice
  He/She/It says ____. Dice «____».
  they say dicen
  What does ____ say? ¿Qué dice ____?
school la escuela
search busca *(command)*
secretary el secretario, la secretaria
See you later! Hasta la vista.; ¡Hasta luego!
See you soon! ¡Hasta pronto!
See you tomorrow! ¡Hasta mañana!
September septiembre
seven siete
seventeen diecisiete
shape la figura
she ella
sheep la oveja
shirt la camisa
shoes los zapatos
short bajo (-a)
shorts los pantalones cortos
show, to mostrar
  show me muéstrame *(command)*
sing, to cantar
  Let's sing. Vamos a cantar.
sister la hermana
sit down, to sentarse
  sit down siéntate *(command)*
six seis
sixteen dieciséis
skirt la falda
sleep, to dormir
sleepy, to be tener sueño
  I'm sleepy. Tengo sueño.
slowly despacio
small pequeño (-a)
snow, to nevar
  It's snowing. Está nevando.
so-so así, así
  I'm so-so. Estoy así, así.
soccer el fútbol
socks los calcetines
son el hijo
sorry, to be sentir
  I'm very sorry. Lo siento mucho.
speak, to hablar
square el cuadrado
stepbrother el hermanastro
stepfather el padrastro
stepmother la madrastra
stepsister la hermanastra
stop! ¡alto!
street la calle
student desk el pupitre
summer el verano
sun el sol
  It's sunny. Hace sol.
Sunday el domingo
sunglasses las gafas de sol
sweater el suéter
swim, to nadar
swimming la natación
swimming pool la piscina

T

table la mesa
take, to tomar
  take toma *(command)*
take away quita *(command)*
take a trip, to hacer un viaje
talk, to hablar
  I'm talking on the telephone. Hablo por teléfono.
tall alto (-a)
teacher la maestra, el maestro
telephone el teléfono
ten diez
tennis el tenis
Thank you. Gracias.
the el, la, los, las
their su, sus
there is, there are hay
think, to pensar
  I'm thinking of . . . Estoy pensando en . . .
thirteen trece
thirty treinta
  thirty-one . . . thirty-nine treinta y uno . . . treinta y nueve
this esta, este, esto
  What's this? ¿Qué es?
this one ésta, éste
three tres
through por
Thursday el jueves
to a, hasta
today hoy
  Today is ____. Hoy es ____.
  What day is today? ¿Qué día es hoy?
tomorrow mañana
  See you tomorrow. Hasta mañana.
  Tomorrow is ____. Mañana es ____.
too también
touch, to tocar
  touch toca *(command)*
traffic light el semáforo
train el tren
triangle el triángulo
trip el viaje
  to take a trip hacer un viaje
T-shirt la camiseta
Tuesday el martes
twelve doce
twenty veinte
  twenty-one . . . twenty-nine veintiuno . . . veintinueve
two dos

U

until hasta
ugly feo (-a)

very muy
very well muy bien

wait espera *(command)*
walking, by foot a pie
  wear, to llevar
  he/she/it is wearing lleva
  I'm wearing llevo
  What are you wearing? ¿Qué llevas?
  you're wearing llevas
weather el tiempo
  The weather is bad. Hace mal tiempo.
  The weather is good. Hace buen tiempo.

What's the weather today? ¿Qué tiempo hace hoy?

Wednesday el miércoles

week la semana

well bien

I'm well Estoy bien.

very well muy bien

what? ¿cómo? ¿qué? ¿cuál?

What are you doing? ¿Qué haces?

What are you going to do? ¿Qué vas a hacer? ¿Qué va a hacer usted?

What's he (she) going to do? ¿Qué va a hacer?

What's missing? ¿Cuál falta?

What's the date? ¿Qué fecha es hoy?

What a pity! ¡Qué lástima!

What a shame! ¡Qué lástima!

when? ¿cuándo?

When is your birthday? ¿Cuándo es tu (su) cumpleaños?

where? ¿dónde?

Where are ____? ¿Dónde están ____?

Where are you going? ¿Adónde vas? ¿Adónde va usted?

Where's ____? ¿Dónde está ____?

which? ¿qué?, ¿cuál?

Which (one) is missing? ¿Cuál falta?

white blanco (-a)

who que, quien

who? ¿quién?

Who has ____? ¿Quién tiene ____?

Who is it? ¿Quién es?

wind el viento

It's windy. Hace viento.

window la ventana

with con

year el año

I'm ____ years old. Tengo ____ años.

yellow amarillo (-a)

yes sí

you tú *(familiar);* usted *(formal)*

your tu, tus; su, sus

You're welcome. De nada.

zero cero

zoo el zoológico